FIRST CANADIAN ARMY

VICTORY IN EUROPE
1944–45

FIRST CANADIAN ARMY

VICTORY IN EUROPE
1944–45

SIMON FORTY AND
LEO MARRIOTT

FIREFLY BOOKS

A FIREFLY BOOK

Published by Firefly Books Ltd. 2020
Text © Simon Forty and Leo Marriott
Copyright 2020 © Simon Forty

First printing

Library of Congress Control Number: 2020940487

Library and Archives Canada Cataloguing in Publication
Title: First Canadian Army : victory in Europe, 1944-45 / Simon Forty and Leo Marriott.
Names: Forty, Simon, author. | Marriott, Leo, author.
Description: Includes bibliographical references and index.
Identifiers: Canadiana 20200272780 | ISBN 9780228102717 (hardcover)
Subjects: LCSH: Canada. Canadian Army. Army, First—History—20th century. | LCSH: Canada. Canadian
   Army. Army, First—History—20th century—Pictorial works. | LCSH: World War, 1939-1945—Europe. |
   LCSH: World War, 1939-1945—Europe—Pictorial works.
Classification: LCC D768.153 F67 2020 | DDC 940.54/1271—dc23

Published in Canada by
Firefly Books Ltd.
50 Staples Avenue, Unit 1
Richmond Hill, Ontario
L4B 0A7

Published in the United States by
Firefly Books (U.S.) Inc.
P.O. Box 1338, Ellicott Station
Buffalo, New York
14205

Printed in China

Page 1: *Men of 8th Canadian Infantry Brigade prepare to advance at the start of Operation Goodwood, 18 July 1944.*

Pages 2–3: *Colin Gibson's beautiful 'Remembrance and Renewal' outside the Juno Beach Centre.*

Below: *St-Lambert-sur-Dive – a battlegroup from 4th Canadian Armoured Division under Maj David Currie made up of armour from the South Alberta Regt and infantry from Argyll and Sunderland Highlanders of Canada hold off enemy attacks. Note the Tiger knocked out at right.*

Contents

Preface

Britain and the world owe Canada a great debt for its involvement in World War II. Without Canada, would Britain have been able to propose fighting them on the beaches in 1940? The forces of Empire rallied to the cause but without Canadian support Britain would have struggled from the off. Canada provided men, a secure area for training, a remarkable manufacturing base to produce weapons and vehicles – and, unlike its North American neighbour, didn't hope for the breakup of the British Empire.

After the debacle in France and Scandinavia, battle was taken to the Axis in the air and at sea and the Canadians were in the thick of it: whether flying for the RAF or in No 6 Group, RCAF, 44 Canadian squadrons were formed. At sea, where the convoys from the New World provided Britain's lifeline, the RCN – the Canadian Navy – also played a significant role.

However, it was with its army that, perhaps, the most obvious assistance came. Involved in home defence in the UK from as early as spring 1940, after Dunkirk Canadian troops were in the front line in Sussex and Kent. Blooded in the Mediterranean, 3rd Canadian Infantry Division assaulted the beaches of Normandy alongside the British as part of Montgomery's 21st Army Group. The Canadians got closer to achieving their D-Day goals than any other of the Allies and had to face determined armoured counter-attacks that they overcame with interest.

333 days later, when the Germans finally ended the slaughter with unconditional surrender, First Canadian Army stood on the shores of the North Sea and, through the efforts of the 1st Canadian Parachute Battalion, the Baltic.

There were criticisms of tactics and alacrity, but these could be laid at every army's door. It was during the 1970s and 1980s that the pernicious myth took hold that the Allies in general, and the British and Canadians specifically, weren't really up to it, that the Germans army outfought them but were crushed by numbers and that the Allies had to rely on artillery to see them through.

I've never understood why so much time has been spent on this proposition. There are undoubtedly moments in the campaign when things could have been done better, but war is an imprecise science. In the end what is more surprising is for how long young men were prepared to put up with it, particularly the infantry. Reading eyewitness acounts of the awful attritional battles – Normandy itself, the Scheldt, the Maas, the Ardennes in the coldest winter of the period, the Reichswald – the bravery of the everyday soldier is incredible. And the amazing thing is that – unlike the Germans whose political elements used capital punishment and threats to offenders' families to keep men in the front line – the Allies ranks were filled with volunteers and conscripts who performed their duties far from home.

Many still rest where they fought: 1,003 Canadian officers and 11,546 other ranks died in north-west Europe. Overall, First Canadian Army's casualties totalled nearly 50,000. They died to rid Europe and the world of a despicable regime.

This book provides a brief pictorial coverage of the events and locations of this period of history, mentioning some of what can be seen today – the memorials, museums and military equipment on the ground.

Opposite: *Canada's first action. German soldiers examine one of the Calgary Regiment's Churchills on the beach at Dieppe. The tanks had arrived late beacause of a navigational error and while many – at least six and possibly as many as nine – had problems with the pebbly beach, 15 of the 27 that landed (two others drowned) made it over the sea wall. The official German report was unimpressed with what was, at that time, Britain's latest tank – although none had been penetrated by anti-tank fire until the guns were moved closer, and then only two. Later versions – including the Churchill AVREs – provided significant support to the troops landing on D-Day. Note the multitude of markings on the tank:*

- *the 175 for the Calgary Regt (on a square divided horizontally, dark blue at top, brown at bottom), the 14th Army Tank Regt, the first Canadian armoured unit ever to enter action.*
- *the maple leaf at right (the 1st Army Tank Bde formation sign was a black square with a gold maple leaf with the silhouette of a ram in the leaf).*

- *the tank's name ('Bert'). Its commander was Squadron Sergeant-Major Gerry M. Menzies – there's a photo of him being forced to surrender. All but three of the Calgaries' crew survivors were taken prisoner because the tanks that were able to do so returned to the beach to cover the withdrawal, and provided covering fire till the last. In total the regiment lost 2 officers and 10 ORs killed and 15 officers and 142 ORs taken prisoner. Only three men returned to England.*
- *the 6 in a square (it would have been a white number on a black background inside a light-blue square to show tank 6 in B Squadron – the square – of the junior regiment in the brigade – red for senior, yellow for middle, blue for junior).*
- *and, of course, the numberplate*

'Bert' reached the promenade, was disabled by shell fire, which broke a track, but was later repaired by the Germans and used to haul other vehicles off the beach. (See also pp12–13.)

Introduction

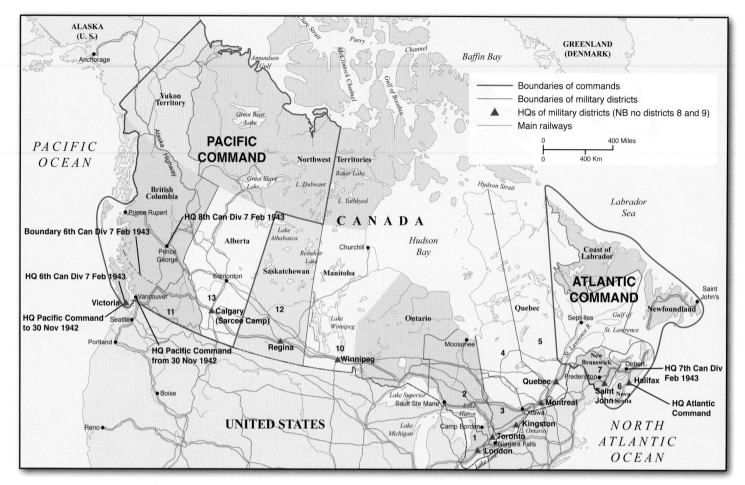

Britain did not stand alone and defenceless in 1940. When France fell and the British Expeditionary Force straggled back to England from the beaches of Dunkirk, Britain's dominions and Commonwealth stood at hand, as they had done in World War I. Britain declared war on Germany not just as a sovereign nation but as the head of the British Commonwealth. Internal politics, the wish for independence and local defence needs may have meant this support was not absolutely complete, but without it Britain is unlikely to have played any significant role in the battles ahead. The glory of the British Empire may have been fading, but it was the largest power bloc in the world at the time and provided a real threat to the Axis and its interests. Not only that, but the forces of empire if not completely integrated with those of Britain, were certainly trained, equipped and led in such a way that cooperation was – relatively – painless and units from anywhere in the empire could fight alongside each other with few military command or supply difficulties.

The armies of the British Empire had shown their worth in World War I when they had served and died alongside the British Army – over 60,000 Canadians, over 60,000 Australians and nearly 75,000 Indians were killed or died fighting in that war. They would do so again in World War II. Without them it is unlikely there would have been British victories in the North African desert, India, the Mediterranean and northwest Europe. In every theatre, Commonwealth troops played a vital role.

The contribution of Canada and the Canadian armed forces to Britain's immediate survival and continued ability to square up to the Axis was crucial. Canadian naval and air involvement – exemplified by No 6 Group, RCAF based in Yorkshire and the RCN's Atlantic convoy protection that helped keep Britain's lifeline with the New World open – were hugely significant. Canada would end the war with the third largest navy in the world and the fourth largest air force. The RCAF was also important for its involvement with the British Commonwealth Air Training Plan/Empire Air Training Scheme: nearly 100 flying schools in Canada at which aircrew from all over the British Empire trained. And then there was Canada's remarkable turnround of industrial power as it went from the struggle to rebuild after the Great Depression to powerhouse of empire, producing everything from tanks to tugs, small arms to synthetic rubber. Canadian manufacturers produced more trucks and lorries than the entire wartime output of the Axis powers.

Men from the Canadian Army started to arrive in Britain in late 1939 and by summer 1940 they were in southern England providing what would have been front-line defence against invasion. The growth in their numbers saw first, on 24 December 1940, the creation of the Canadian Corps and then, in April 1942, the creation of First Canadian Army with two corps, the existing, unnumbered, unit becoming I Canadian Corps. The latter finally became operational in Italy and fought there until the beginning of 1945 with various Commonwealth units under command.

Left: *Military organisation of Canada during World War II. Most of the training for Canadian forces in Europe was undertaken in Atlantic Command and two locations in particular stand out: Halifax, the major port through which Canadian troops boarded troopships for the UK, and Debert Military Camp. The original facility at Debert was considerably increased in 1940 until it was capable of accommodating units up to divisional size. There over 300,000 soldiers trained before they left for service overseas. The nearby RCAF Station Debert was an important part of the British Commonwealth Air Training Plan.*

Above Right: *At Halifax, infantrymen of the Toronto Scottish Regiment board* HM Troopship Empress of Australia *bound for Britain, 7 December 1939.*

Below and Right: *The first Canadian-built tank – a Valentine – emerges from Angus Shops of the Canadian Pacific Railway, 27 May 1941 Canadian vehicle production, particularly of trucks and wheeled vehicles, played a major role in the Allied victory.*

Right: *Iceland was ruled by King Christian X of Denmark. Sitting at a crucial strategic location commanding the Denmark Strait in the middle of the Atlantic routes between North America and the United Kingdom, Iceland was too important to British interests to allow it to fall into German hands. In spite of its declared neutrality, when the Germans had occupied Denmark in April 1940 Britain took steps to ensure that Iceland remained in Allied hands. On 10 May 1940 in Operation Fork a force of 746 men under Col Robert Sturges invaded and occupied the island. On 17 May the first Canadian troops reached the island and most British left. For almost a year Canadians occupied Iceland until they, too, left. Shortly after, the United States took over from the British garrison – starting a friendly US invasion that would endure until 2006. This is a US soldier on guard duty.*

When constituted, First Canadian Army was led by Lt Gen A.G.L. 'Andy' McNaughton – a decorated World War I artilleryman who was known for his technical innovations, intellect, dislike of conscription and bias towards officers with a scientific bent. He was a talented man who had many abilities and the obvious choice to command the Canadian Expeditionary Force in Britain and First Canadian Army when it was created.

McNaughton also had his defects. Intellectually it may have made sense while he was Chief of the Canadian Defence Staff (1929–35) to save money by abolishing the RCN; practically, it was a nonsense that didn't happen but did lead to a fault line between the two services that took a long time to mend. He was also a better artilleryman than army commander as was proved decisively during Exercise Spartan in Britain 4–12 March 1943. Fairly or unfairly – and one must never forget that politics play a part in all such decisions – British CIGS and chairman of the Chiefs of Staff Committee decided he was unfit to command an army during wartime. He was replaced by Lt Gen H.D.G. 'Harry' Crerar, who would command until the end of the war.

Crerar was, at the time, the most experienced field commander in the Canadian Army, having commanded I Canadian Corps in Italy when, finally, McNaughton had been pushed into letting the Canadian forces be used as part of Eighth Army. Until then – as Pershing had with US forces during World War I – McNaughton had done everything he could to ensure that Canadian units were not used piecemeal. That, however, was just how they would be used until First Canadian Army became operational in Normandy in July 1944.

The Canadian Army had seen little action since 1939 and most of that had been bloody. In December 1941, some 2,000 Canadians fought against the Japanese attack on Hong Kong. Under Brig J.K. Lawson, the Royal Rifles of Canada and Winnipeg Grenadiers arrived a month before the Japanese and had little time for acclimatisation – their vehicles hadn't even arrived. They had reached Manila when the Japanese attack on Pearl Harbor took place, and the Americans were allowed to requisition them.

Continued on p15.

THE CANADIAN ARMY IN WORLD WAR II

Over 730,000 Canadians served in the Canadian Army and half went overseas. In 1940, 1st Canadian Inf Bde went to Brittany as a part of the second British Expeditionary Force but its stay was limited. From May 1940 small units garrisoned Jamaica, Bermuda and Nassau in the West Indies, and from May 1940 to mid-1941, Iceland. From 1940, Canadian troops helped with British Home Defence – they would have been in the front line if a German invasion had taken place. In all, eight Canadian divisions were raised during the war, the following seeing service overseas:

1st Infantry: fought in Sicily, Italy and with First Canadian Army.

2nd Infantry: first saw action during Operation Jubilee (Dieppe) and, after reconstruction, with Second British Army during the battle of Normandy. It went on to fight with First Canadian Army along the Channel coast, including the Scheldt clearance, before being part of the liberation of the Netherlands.

3rd Infantry: Assaulted Juno Beach on D-Day as part of Second British Army before passing to Canadian First Army, fighting along the Channel, clearing Breskens Pocket, and on into the Netherlands.

4th Armoured: formed out of 4th Inf Div in 1942 fought in battle of Normandy, Breskens Pocket, the Netherlands and Germany.

5th Armoured: redesignated from 1st Armd, fought in Italy and, in 1945, in Germany.

6th Infantry: raised in 1942, in 1943 a brigade went to the Aleutians but didn't see action; returned to Canada.

Left: *Infantrymen of C Coy, Royal Rifles of Canada, disembarking from HMCS Prince Robert in Hong Kong, 16 November 1941. The RRC and the Winnipeg Grenadiers left from Vancouver on 27 October 1941 and swelled the existing 12,000-strong garrison by nearly 2,000 soldiers, although the Canadians were relatively untrained. The Japanese attacked on 8 December, bombing Kai Tak airport and crossing the border. The defence of the colony lasted until Christmas Day and cost the Canadians 290 dead and 493 wounded. A further 264 would die in captivity. Canadian troops sent to Hong Kong were issued hot weather uniforms, Canada long having used these uniforms within the country itself during the summer months for its Permanent Force. These uniforms were made of light green twilled cotton and it seems likely that the men deployed to Hong Kong in 1941 were issued these uniforms. The men waiting to disembark carry packs and kit bags containing their extra items of uniform and personal gear.*

Below Left: *CSM J.R. Osborn of A Coy, Winnipeg Grenadiers seen in Jamaica, in 1940–41. Osborn's unit had been garrisoning the Caribbean island before it was sent to Hong Kong. On 19 December 1941, Osborn was killed in action and was posthumously awarded the Victoria Cross after the war when news of his bravery became known. He had led the charge that retook Mount Butler from the Japanese, but died when his men were forced off, and surrounded. He gave his life to save his men, throwing himself on a grenade before it exploded.*

Canadian infantrymen embarking on landing craft during a exercise before Operation Jubilee. Desperate to see action, the Canadian forces suffered a major reverse at Dieppe: 3,367 of the 5,000 who took part were killed, wounded or taken prisoner.

DIEPPE

I Canadian Corps troops in England, some for nearly two years, were itching for action, none more so than the corps commander, Harry Crerar. They had been kept from involvement in North Africa because Lt Gen McNaughton – understandably – wanted to ensure that the Canadian units stayed together under Canadian command. When Maj Gen Montgomery, under whose South-Eastern Command the Canadians came, offered them the chance to take part in Operation Jubilee, Crerar jumped at it – he had been lobbying for just this opportunity while deputising for McNaughton during the latter's recent illness. Unfortunately, it was a bad choice.

While there's no doubt that the operation provided important experience and crucial lessons on what the Allies would have to improve before they could invade France, there's no getting around the fact that it was a fiasco and many more brave men died than should have done. The men on the beaches fought heroically and VCs were awarded to Capt John Foote (RHLI) and Lt Col Charles Merritt of the South Saskatchewan Regt, the DCM to Pte William A. Haggard (another SSR man) and signaller Sgt David L. Hart received the Military Medal.

There were many legitimate reasons for the operation, particularly that promoted by the RAF which wanted to draw the Luftwaffe into battle and help win air superiority over the French coast, and the Russians who wanted to relieve pressure on the Eastern Front. However, Bomber Command didn't take part and the Royal Navy was unwilling to allow a capital ship either. Consequently, it's difficult to square the results of the raid against the cost: 2nd Can Inf Div, supported by 58 Churchill tanks (only 27 landed) and two Commando units on the flanks, attacked a defended port head on without a preliminary bombardment or major naval assistance. The slaughter that ensued proved that the invasion of France would take much more planning and equipment than was available at the time. Indeed, it scared British planners sufficiently for them to argue against American wishes for an invasion in 1943. That negative was probably the most positive result of the raid.

There are many memorials in Dieppe remembering the events of 19 August 1942.

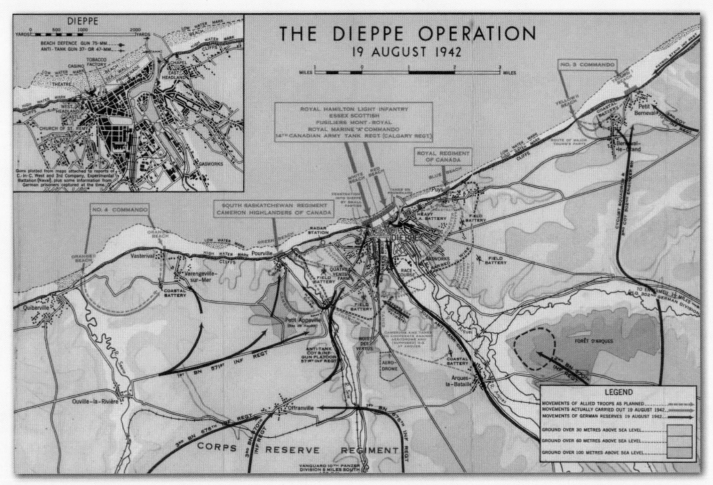

THE DIEPPE OPERATION
19 AUGUST 1942

Above and Below: *The major lesson of Dieppe was 'the need for overwhelming fire support, including close support, during the initial stages of the attack'. This meant a heavy air attack, a naval bombardment much heavier than anything attempted at Dieppe, and special support craft for inshore work. Other important lessons concerned the shingle beach that caused so many problems for the vehicles that were landed. In future, advance knowledge of likely invasion beaches was garnered by the Combined Ops Assault Pilotage Parties, men in canoes who clandestinely surveyed the beaches and their defences. Note the wading pipes on the engine back. By 6 June 1944 these had become more sophisticated. (See p43.)*

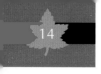

Canadian soldiers were rushed across the Atlantic to help defend Britain. The first arrived in December 1939 and by December 1940 there were sufficient to form the Canadian Corps. Commanded by Lt Gen McNaughton it became operational on 24 December 1940 based at Headley Court in Surrey. The build-up of Canadian troops continued apace and on 6 April 1942 First Canadian Army and a second Canadian Corps were created. As we all know, the prospective German invasion of Britain didn't happen in summer 1940. The 'miracle of Dunkirk', failure to defeat the RAF over southern England and – more importantly – the strength of the Royal Navy all helped convince Hitler his army would be better employed elsewhere: his eyes turned to Russia. The Canadian forces in Britain embarked on what for some would be many years of training.

Above Right: *A wet two-day exercise for units of the 1st Can Inf Div in spring 1941. They wear typical cold weather clothing for the early part of the war. The Canadian greatcoat was made in the same greenish shade as the battledress and was a double-breasted garment with two rows of Canadian general service buttons up the front. A vent and half belt at the rear allowed it to be expanded when worn over layers of clothing. The officer leading from the front wears a waterproof mackintosh-style coat that was common amongst officers throughout the Empire in the early stages of the war.*

Centre Right: *Gunners of the 2nd Anti-Tank Regt, RCA practising river crossing during an exercise near Bognor Regis, on 14 December 1942. Their 37-pattern webbing is clearly visible. Canadian-produced webbing was more yellowish when new than that manufactured by other Empire nations and was regarded as the best quality of all the countries' production. It is interesting to note that the haversack for the respirator has been slung to the rear so it is not encumbering the troops, rather than being worn in the more usual 'alert' position, high on the chest.*

Right: *HM King George VI reviews the South Saskatchewan Regt, 17 July 1943, Whitley Camp, Sussex. They wear skeleton webbing, without ammunition pouches, Canadian-produced battledress – greener in hue than British-made uniforms and of a smoother, higher quality fabric – and Canadian-produced boots that lack a toecap and resemble the World War I-pattern.*

Left: *Machine gunners of the Saskatoon Light Infantry at Potenza, Italy, on 20 September 1943. The venerable Vickers (water-cooled: note water tube and can attached) was the MMG for all British and Commonwealth forces. Canadian units fought with Eighth Army in Italy enduring the difficult terrain and weather until Operation Goldflake took them back to northwest Europe where they joined First Canadian Army in the final push against Germany. Canadian troops in Italy were issued tan-coloured khaki-drill uniforms from a variety of sources including British, Canadian and Indian. Some was US War Aid-produced. The clothing was lightweight and comfortable in the Italian sun, with shirts often made from an open-weave Aertex fabric that allowed air to the skin. The left-hand gunner of this team wears an armoured fighting vehicle crewman's helmet, with its distinctive rimless shape. The same shell was used by airborne troops and dispatch riders, but only the AFV version had this simple chin strap.*

Lawson's men joined 12,000 Colonial troops: two British battalions (2/Royal Scots – infantry and 1/Middlesex Regiment – MG), two Indian (5/7th Rajput and 2/14th Punjab Regiments (both infantry), Chinese, artillery and engineer units. They were distributed on the mainland (the 'Gin Drinker's Line') and the island itself. On 11 December 1941, D Coy of the Winnipeg Grenadiers fired the first Canadian shots in action in World War II. That same day the Gin Drinker's Line fell and the defenders retreated in good order back to Hong Kong island. Besieged, without hope of relief, without air or sea assets, the Commonwealth forces held out for 17 days of constant fighting before surrendering on Christmas Day. The survivors entered a hellish captivity and many died.

After Hong Kong and the raid on Dieppe, the next significant action for Canadian troops was in North Africa but not as part of Operation Torch, the first large-scale Allied amphibious landings. During the Tunisian campaign that followed, 201 Canadian officers and 147 NCOs were given the opportunity to reinforce First British Army units, replacing casualties. Four officers and four NCOs died in the process but the experience gained would prove hugely helpful in the campaigns that followed, the first in the Mediterranean.

Before then, there was a change in policy. Gen McNaughton wanted Canadians to fight together as a national unit. The authorities in Ottawa felt that the time had come for action in any form and allowed 1st Can Inf Div – commanded by Maj Gen G.G. 'Guy' Simonds – and 1st Can Army Tank Bde (later the 1st Can Armd Bde) to take part in the invasion of Sicily as part of Eighth (BR) Army's XXX Corps commanded by Lt Gen Oliver Leese.

It didn't start particularly well. Enemy submarines sank three ships in the convoy to Sicily killing 55 Canadians along with 500 vehicles and artillery pieces which would be much missed. However, the Canadian contingent performed well in its first campaign although it did not come through its baptism of fire unscathed: 2,434 casualties and 38 officers and 447 ORs dead.

After Sicily HQ I Canadian Corps – under General Crerar – and 5th Canadian Armd Div both moved to Italy with Eighth Army as the split in Canada's overseas military contingent left First Canadian Army and II Canadian Corps HQs along with two divisions and an armoured brigade in England and II Canadian Corps in Italy. On 26 December 1943 Gen McNaughton left England and General Kenneth Stuart took over for an interim period.

In Italy, Crerar's I Canadian Corps had become operational in November 1943, but it wasn't until Operation Diadem in May 1944 that it fought as a corps. Before then, 1st Can Inf Div and 1st Can Armd Bde had fought as part of Eighth British Army, and it was while part of V (BR) Corps that Canadian troops fought the battle of Ortona between 20 and 28 December 1943.

Ortona saw the Canadians up against the paratroopers of the 1. Fallschirmjäger-Division in a desperate house-to-house, hand-to-hand battle. The casualties were sizeable, but the Canadians made sure that even in the middle of the carnage they celebrated Christmas. Col C.P. Stacey, director of Canada's Historical Section, General Staff and the most important Canadian military writer of his generation, recorded in the *Official Historical Summary*: 'Tables were actually laid with white cloths, and the four rifle companies

Continued on p18.

Although separate from the Canadian Army it's worth remembering the part the RCAF played within the RAF's Bomber Command. Among its squadrons was No 425 – the first French-Canadian Squadron, its lark emblem giving it the nickname, 'Les Alouettes.' Its motto was '*Je te plumerai*' (I shall pluck you). Formed in Britain on 25 June 1942 as part of No 4 Group, RAF Bomber Command, operating Wellingtons, on 1 January 1943 the squadron transferred to No 6 (RCAF) Group. After supporting the invasions of Sicily and Italy, in October 1943 the squadron returned to Britain, converting to the Halifax as seen here.

*These photos (**Right** and **Below**) of No 425 Squadron were taken at its home, RAF Tholthorpe, on 23 November 1944. There's a memorial on the village green (**Opposite, Above Left**). The airfield was one of ten used by No 6 Group, whose HQ was at Allerton Park, northwest of York.*

THE ROYAL CANADIAN AIR FORCE (RCAF)

Above: *Andrew Charles (Andy) Mynarski, VC (14 October 1916–3 June 1944) was a Canadian recipient of the Victoria Cross. Mynarski was 27 years old and flew with No 419 'Moose' Squadron, RCAF when he gave his life attempting to help rescue a trapped crew member on a mission. His VC was awarded in 1946, the last such award to a Canadian airman in World War II. This memorial is situated in front of the old Officers Mess now the George Hotel near Teeside Airport.*

Left: *There are only two Lancaster bombers still flying. This one belongs to the Canadian Warplane Heritage Museum in Hamilton, Ontario. It is known as the Mynarski Memorial Lancaster in honour of Pilot Officer Mynarski, and is painted in the markings of his aircraft.*

Right: *Lt Gen Oliver Leese, GOC British Eighth Army (right) in discussion with Maj Gen Eedson L.M. Burns, GOC I Canadian Corps during Operation Diadem (started 11 May 1944) in Italy. The operation saw the Allies break through the Hitler Line and thus relieve pressure on the beleaguered forces at Anzio. Note the Maple Leaf vehicle marking on the Daimler Dingo scout car. If the backing colour is red it would denote 1st Can Inf Div; if maroon, 5th Armd Div. The Canadians would be united with those fighting in northwest Europe in 1945 by Operation Goldflake.*

Opposite, Above and Below Left: *Getting the medical setup right for the invasion and in the field.*

Opposite, Below Right: *The boss. Gen (Later FM) Sir Bernard Law Montgomery was a difficult man to like and postwar many have tried to dismiss his abilities without looking at the constraints under which he had to work. Be that as it may, he did his job: he planned the invasion and won the battle of Normandy.*

were relieved in succession, each for two hours, for the festivities.' Around them, a quarter of the Canadian casualties in the whole of the Italian campaign were sustained in this one epic battle.

In March 1944 Crerar took over as commander of First Canadian Army, returning from Italy where he left Lt Gen Eedson Burns commanding I Canadian Corps, and Stuart moved to become Chief of Staff at Canadian Military HQ in England. After 20 months in Italy, in February–March 1945, Operation Goldflake moved Canadian troops in Italy secretly to the Netherlands. There had been 1,626 officers and 23,638 other ranks casualties; of these, as Stacey records, '420 officers and 5,379 other ranks slept in Italian soil.'

Crerar reached England as preparations for the invasion of Normandy were at an advanced stage. Having learnt lessons at Dieppe, the training emphasised the importance of the pre-invasion bombardment – including artillery firing from landing craft as they approached the shore and DD swimming tanks – specialised equipment to help men and vehicles off the beaches (much of this to be provided by 'Hobart's funnies', the flails, AVREs, bridge and roadway layers of 79th (BR) Armd Div) a significant naval warship presence and the essential procurement of air superiority over the beaches, all this to be followed by a build-up of men and anti-tank weapons that would be able to withstand the inevitable enemy counter-attacks and allow the bridgehead to widen sufficiently for airstrips to be created. And Canadian troops would be in the lead.

79TH ARMOURED DIVISION

Led by Maj Gen Sir Percy Hobart, the 79th was originally formed as a standard armoured division but became the testbed for a range of specialised equipment designed specifically to help the invasion of Europe. The vehicles continued to be used throughout the campaign in northwest Europe. The main components on D-Day were:

• Sherman Crabs – anti-mine flail tanks developed and used in North Africa on the Matilda chassis. By D-Day Shermans had replaced them.

• Churchill AVRE – armed with a bunker-busting 290mm spigot mortar (the Petard) the Armoured Vehicle Royal Engineers was the mainstay of the RE assault squadrons, two of which accompanied each of the infantry divisions on Gold, Juno and Sword beaches to breach sea walls or bridge them, remove beach obstacles and clear the way for the infantry. They accomplished this in the main, although with considerable losses. AVREs could also be fitted with other equipment to surmount obstacles such as anti-tank ditches or walls. These included fascines – bundles of wood and pipes to fill ditches or trenches; bridging equipment (particularly the small box girder bridge); and the Bobbin carpet layer to lay matting on soft sand.

Principal Canadian static medical installations in the UK 1939–1946

Canadian Hospitals as at 15 May 1944

Aldershot	No 4 Can General
Alton	No 1 Can Special
Alton	Convalescent (dormant)
Basingstoke	Neurological
Bordon	No 1 Can Med Centre
Bramshott	No 2 Can General
Cherry Tree	No 18 Can General
Colchester	Roman Way Convalescent
Cove	No 4 Can Med Centre
Cranleigh	Alderbrook Park Convalescent
Cuckfield	No 13 Can General
Horley	No 12 Can General
Horsham	No 9 Can General
Leavesden	No 20 Can General
Marston Green	No 19 Can General
Pinewood	No 17 Can General
Rushmoor	No 3 Can Med Centre
Staunton on Wye	Massey Foundation Convalescent
Taplow	No 11 Can General
Welwyn	Digswell Place Convalescent
Witley	No 2 Can Med Centre

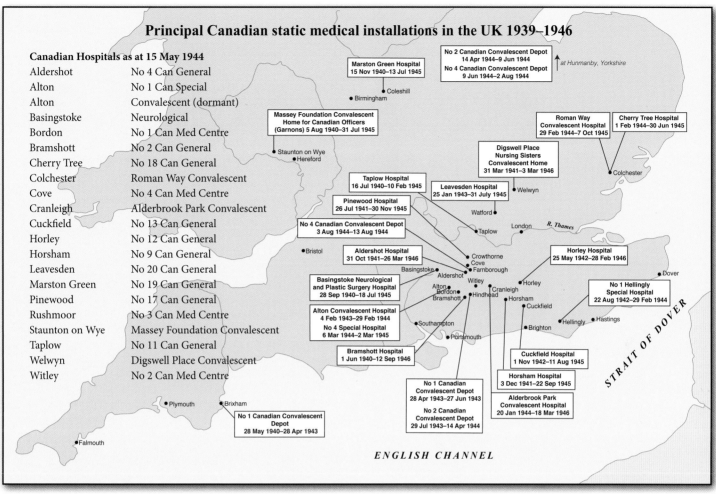

ENGLISH CHANNEL

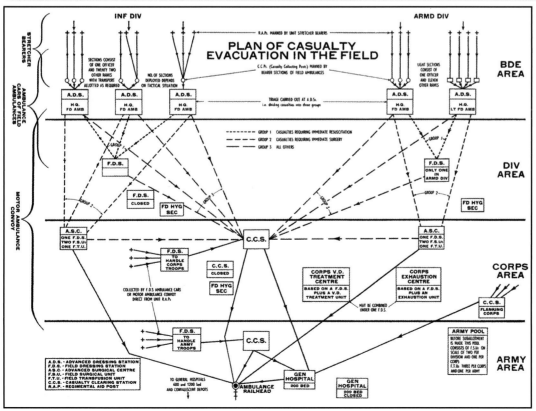

Anyone who says that the British and Canadian forces who landed on D-Day were underprepared cannot have been watching! From 1942 onwards, with increasing verisimilitude, the troops trained. However, the problem was not how much training they had done but how they had been trained. Fundamental flaws in British tactical approaches to the use of infantry, its cooperation with tanks and Montgomery's artillery-led approach to battle meant that 21st Army Group did not always perform with the tactical alacrity expected of it. Strategically, however, the Allies had the upper hand and no amount of tactical knowledge could save the German armour from having to react piecemeal to Monty's 'colossal cracks' approach.

Left: *Headquarters of the Governor General's Horse Guards during Exercise Snaffle, Sussex, 10 August 1943.*

Below Left: *Infantrymen of the 3rd Can Inf Div scaling a cliff during an assault course, Seaford, 21 July 1942.*

Below: *An exercise on Salisbury Plain, 6 February 1944.*

Opposite, Above Left: *RN beach commandos aboard an LCA of the 529th Flotilla, RN, during another exercise, 9 May 1944.*

Opposite, Above Right: *Men of the 1st Bn, the Canadian Scottish Regiment, in an LCA during the dress rehearsal for the D-Day landings, Exercise Fabius, 29 April–4 May 1944.*

Opposite, Below: *Infantry train on an RCN landing craft infantry (large), May 1944.*

Right: *As the big day approached, vehicles were waterproofed – a difficult task on a tank whose underside rivets had to be filled and coated, and closer to embarkation, extension breathers had to be attached to engine air intakes and exhausts.*

Below Right and Below: *The 3rd Can Inf Div HQ moved to Balmer Lawn near Beaulieu – closer to the division's embarkation points on Stokes Bay. In 2016, Lt Col Simon Rushen of the Royal Canadian Regt and veteran Cpl Bob Roberts, who stormed ashore on Nan Red Beach on D-Day with the North Shore Regt, planted a maple tree at today's Balmer Lawn hotel to remember the Canadians stationed here.*

This Maple, planted in 2016 is in memory of all Canadians stationed here in 1944. Their sacrifice will not be forgotten

Sponsored by Bashley Plant Centre

The 3rd Can Inf Div constituted Assault Force J, heading for Juno Beach. Many troops boarded in Southampton itself or berthed there before moving out into the Solent. The boarding was practised during Exercise Fabius in early May 1944 as shown in this photo (**Centre Right**) of North Nova Scotia Highlanders aboard LCI(L) 135 *at Town Quay. The distinctive dome belongs to the 1925 Harbour Board offices (***Below** and **B** on the modern photo). This photo (**Above Right** at **A** below) shows the real thing: Southampton's Ocean Dock on 4 June. Amongst the AFVs visible are two Fireflies (second back on left). Heading for Nan White serial 1409 is LCT5 2436 carrying a 22nd Dragoons' Sherman Crab, two AVREs of 80th Assault Sqn, RE (note the fascine) and a D7 armoured bulldozer of 26th Assault Sqn, RE.*

Above: *This wonderful painting by Colin M. Baxter of one of the hards at Stokes Bay provides a realistic view of the embarkation with the fleet anchored in the Solent and the hills of the Isle of Wight behind. Note the dolphin tethering point at right and the concrete 'chocolate block' matting, some of which is still visible today at low tide. LCT-1092 is a Mk 4 LCT – the most numerous mark, 865 units were built by the British. It hit a mine and foundered while under tow on 10 August 1944. Note the Austin 6 x 4 with a Coles Mark VI Crane at right – Courseulles was operating as a port by D+3, the 1033rd and 1034th Port Operating Companies having landed on Juno, and they used RB10 and RB19 cranes. They also got the coast railway running using captured German stock. A French bucket-dredge found at Courseulles was used to help get other ports at Isigny, Grandcamp and St-Vaast.*

Right: *There's a memorial on Stokes Bay to the Canadians who boarded for Normandy.*

Below: *Stokes Bay on a grey summer's morning much like those on 5 and 6 June 1944.*

Right and Below: *Stormont, Dundas and Glengarry Highlanders and Highland Light Infantry of Canada going aboard landing craft on 4 June. Serials 1706–1711 were scheduled to take the troops to Nan Red but were diverted to Nan White Beach and were also delayed for almost an hour. The LCI(L)s were built in the United States and could carry around 200 men. HMCS LCI(L)-250, with its shark's teeth artwork seen (**Below**) alongside HMCS LCI(L)-125, had an incident-packed 6 June, carrying 180 men (and 120 folding bicycles) of the Highland Light Infantry of Canada's B Coy and Bn HQ along with two men from D Section, 4th Canadian Provost Coy. LCI(L)-250 hit a mine on the port bow and then lost both its ramps while getting off the beach. In doing so it rammed and further damaged LCI(L)-118, which had also felt the effects of the mine).*

Right: *Motor torpedo boats were the sports cars of the seas, crafted from plywood, carrying 2,500 gallons of 100% octane fuel and armed to the teeth with torpedoes, MGs, 20mm Oerlikons, and 40mm Pom-Poms or 6pdr guns. Two RCN flotillas came under Dover Command during the invasion—the 29th (the 'Fighting Sea Fleas') and the 65th. Both played an important role, protecting the flanks from E-boats and other attackers, even destroyers on occasions. These Fairmile MTBs, some from the 65th Flotilla, RCN are at Great Yarmouth.*

Centre and Below Right: *HMCS Algonquin was directly involved during D-Day. Here (**Below Right**), crew of one of its 4.7-inch guns pile shell cases and sponge out the gun after bombarding German shore defences.*

Below: *The RCN provided a significant presence during the invasion – including the destroyers Algonquin and Sioux, LSI(M)s Prince David (seen on a May 1944 exercise) and Prince Henry, as well as three flotillas of LCI(L)s – 30 in total.*

Opposite: *HM LCI(L)-125 was commissioned into the Royal Navy through Lend-Lease and, manned by a Canadian crew, delivered A Coy, and 1st Pl, D Coy of the Highland Light Infantry of Canada onto Nan White Beach at high tide on D-Day. These were follow-up troops of 9th Inf Bde, the reserve brigade. LCI(L)-125 sustained bow damage and a list that had to be corrected by flooding. Here the port-side gangway is deployed allowing the men and their bicycles to disembark. (See also p25.) Note the waterproofing used by some to protect their rifles.*

1 D-Day, 6 June 1944

With all the tales of heroism and bravery, it's all too easy to forget how awful it must have been on the beaches on D-Day. For the defenders, some of them eastern Europeans coerced into fighting for the Third Reich, others young recruits, others older men or those recovering from wounds, it must have been hellish: an aerial bombardment followed by shelling from the Allied heavy warships and then the artillery on the landing craft, a salvo of rockets and finally, appearing from the sea the deadly surprise of swimming tanks.

For the attackers, the choppy seas and rolling landing craft induced seasickness, not helped by nerves and fear, and the closer the boats got to shore so the enemy's underwater defences – mines, stakes, Czech hedgehogs with shells attached – took their toll. To fall into the sea often meant death by drowning as the weight of equipment – even the soggy mass of that extra carton of cigarettes provided by wellwishers in England – dragged the soldier to a watery grave. And then there were the integrated defences of the Atlantic Wall: minefields that forced attackers into killing zones, casemates that held anti-tank weapons and field guns, open concrete emplacements – known as Tobruks –

MAIN ASSAULT UNITS (CAN AND *BRIT*)

7th Infantry Brigade	8th Infantry Brigade
Royal Winnipeg Rifles	Queen's Own Rifles of Canada
C Coy, 1st Canadian Scottish	Régt de la Chaudière
Regina Rifle Regt	North Shore Regt
B Sqn, 22nd Dragoons (flails)	*B Sqn, 22nd Dragoons (flails)*
6th Armd Regt, 1st Hussars (DDs)	10th Armd Regt, Fort Garry Horse
12th and 13th Field Regts, RCA	(DDs)
(SP artillery)	14th and 19th Field Regts, RCA
A/D Coys, Cameron Highlanders	(SP artillery)
of Ottawa (MGs and mors)	B Coy Cameron Highlanders of
3/2nd (RM) Armd Support Regt	Ottawa (MGs and mors)
94th Bty, 3rd ATk Regt (6pdrs)	*4/2nd (RM) Armd Support Regt*
246th Bty, 62nd ATk Regt (17pdrs)	*105th Bty, 3rd ATk Regt (M10s)*
248th Bty, 62nd ATk Regt (M10s)	*247th Bty, 62nd ATk Regt (17pdrs)*
26th Assault Sqn, RE (AVREs)	*80th Assault Sqn, RE (AVREs)*
5th and 6th Can Field Coy, RCE	5th and 16th Can Field Coy, RCE
7th Beach Group	*8th Beach Group*
+ RCCS, RCAMC, RCEME, RMP	+ RCCS, RCAMC, RCEME, RMP

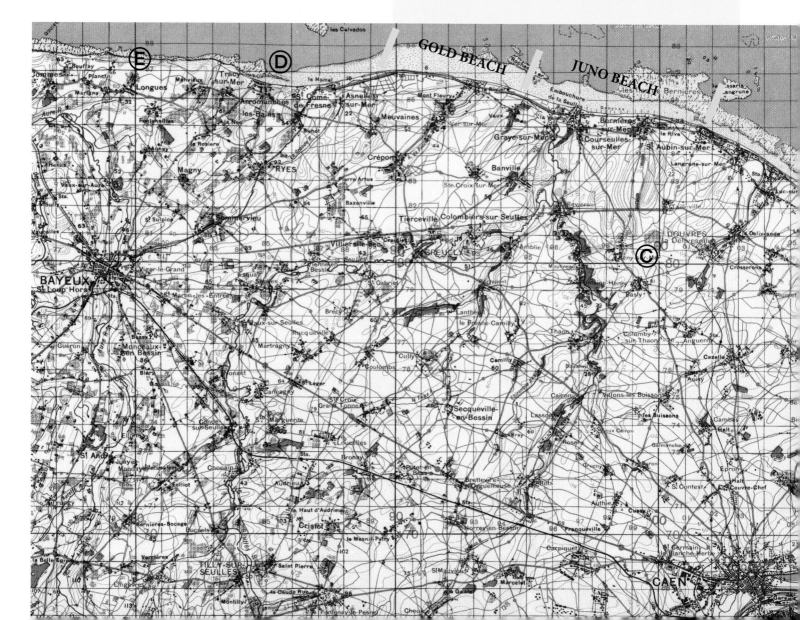

with machine guns and mortars, further inland, heavier batteries and Nebelwerfer. Juno Beach may not have had the defences and geography of Omaha, but it had strongpoints made from linked, fortified houses; beach walls and carefully sited pillboxes.

The Allies, however, had other advantages. Their weather forecasting proved better than that of the Germans who didn't believe the winds and wave heights would allow an invasion. Because of this, Rommel was in Germany and a number of senior commanders were away from their units. Second, the Germans had fallen for the deception of Operation Fortitude hook, line and sinker. They believed that the Pas de Calais was the invasion point and wouldn't commit forces there to Normandy and what they thought was a feint. Third, the Allies had achieved complete air and sea dominance in the area. There would be few ships lost to the Kriegsmarine and few Luftwaffe aircraft over the battlefield. Indeed, there was more chance of blue on blue friendly fire incidents as happened to the Inns of Court Regt at Jerusalem Crossroads near Bayeux when a USAF P-47 fighter-bomber attack destroyed five vehicles and killed a number of men who are buried in the nearby CWGC cemetery.

The fighting on Juno Beach was intense and harder than anywhere else other than Omaha. However, the early arrival of the DD amphibious tanks and other armour finally got through the belt of heavy weapons on the beaches and the extensive areas of barbed wire, anti-tank ditches, mines and flooded marshland, allowing the follow-up troops to advance deeper into Normandy than at any other beach. The fly in the ointment was the radar station at Douvres-la-Délivrande that was much more deeply entrenched than expected and held out until 17 June.

Below Left: *The British and Canadian area: note the bridges over the Orne and Canal de Caen (**A**), taken by coup de main Operation Deadstick; Merville Battery (**B**); the bridges over the Dives knocked out by 6th Airborne (**1** Varaville, **2** Robehomme, **3** Bures, **4** Troarn); the Douvres radar station that took so much dislodging (**C**); Arromanches – the site of the British Mulberry harbour (**D**); and the location of the Longues Battery (**E**).*

Below: *The routes taken on D-Day. The battle of Normandy started on 6 June and by the time Chambois was taken on 19 August, it was all but over. Liberation dates for major locations shown.*

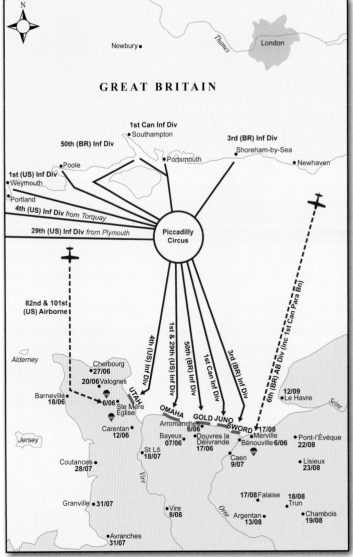

Right: *A heavily loaded RCAF LST leaves Southampton Ocean Dock, the dome of the Harbour Board offices obvious in the background. It shows well the huge amount of materiel that moved from south England to Normandy.*

Below: *Captain S. Mendelsohn, RCA briefing soldiers en route to the beach-head. He wears a Mk III helmet – referred to as turtle-shaped – and the men uninflated life preservers.*

Below Right: *The French were more than happy to be liberated by French-speakers, of which there were many in First Canadian Army – particularly in the traditional French regiments, the Royal 22e, Les Fusiliers Mont-Royal, the Régiment de Maisonneuve and, as here, Le Régiment de la Chaudière, whose Pte Jack Roy prepares to disembark from HMCS* Prince David *off Bernières-sur-Mer. He has a No 38 Wireless Set on his chest, an oilskin anti-gas cape over his arm (they were used as raincoats) and clutches the webbing pouch for his radio antenna.*

Left: *L/Cpl George Gagnon, 14th Field Regt, RCA, fuses No 36M hand grenades aboard the LST that will take him to Normandy. Southampton, 4 June 1944. He's working in a Universal Carrier that has been waterproofed for deep wading – the metal rods are keyed to brackets welded to the hull and the gaps filled with Bostick.*

Below Left: *Another chore for a gunner – LBombardier Walter Cooper counts out 105mm shells which will be fired on D-Day by M7 Priests of 14th Field Regt, RCA.*

Below: *Men line up to enter their LCAs from the deck of HMCS* Prince Henry. *A number wear their gas capes as raincoats.*

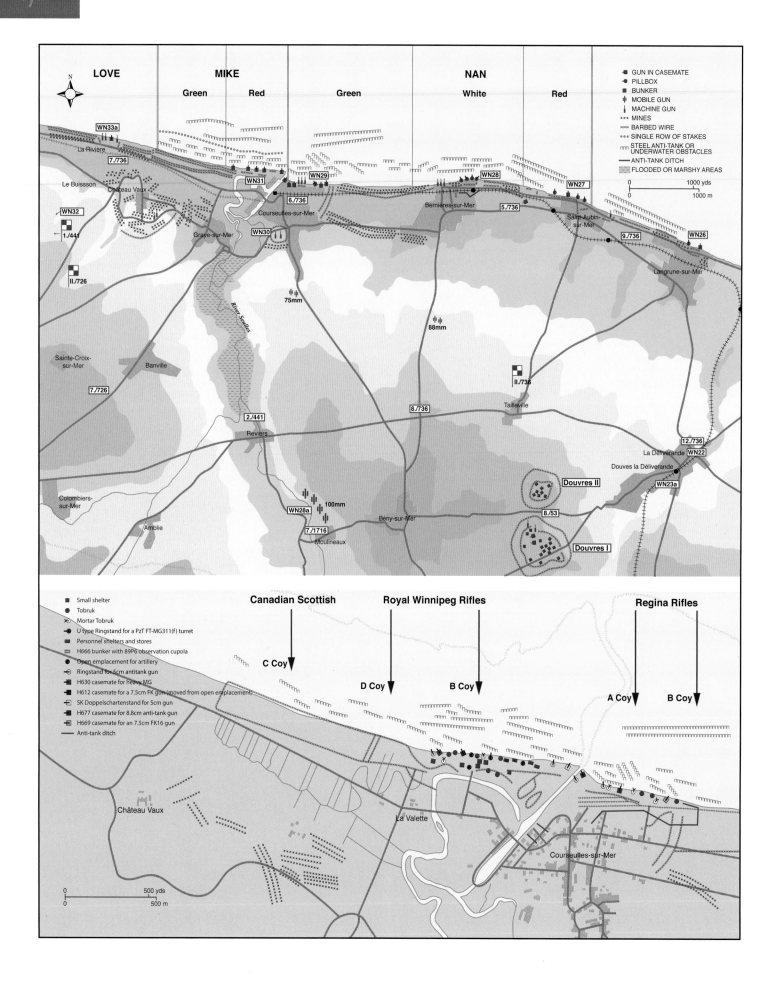

LOVE

MIKE

Green   Red   Green

NAN

White   Red

GUN IN CASEMATE
PILLBOX
BUNKER
MOBILE GUN
MACHINE GUN
MINES
BARBED WIRE
SINGLE ROW OF STAKES
STEEL ANTI-TANK OR UNDERWATER OBSTACLES
ANTI-TANK DITCH
FLOODED OR MARSHY AREAS

0   1000 yds
0   1000 m

WN33a
7./736
La Rivière
Le Buissson
Château Vaux
WN32
1./441
II./726
Sainte-Croix-sur-Mer
Banville
7./726
2./441
Reviers
Colombiers-sur-Mer
Amblie
WN28a
100mm
7./1716
Moulineaux
WN31
6./736
Courseulles-sur-Mer
WN30
Graye-sur-Mer
River Seulles
75mm
WN29
88mm
Berniéres-sur-Mer
5./736
II./736
Tailleville
8./736
Bény-sur-Mer
Douvres II
8./53
Douvres I
WN28
WN27
Saint-Aubin-sur-Mer
9./736
WN26
Langrune-sur-Mer
La Délivrande
12./736
WN22
Douves la Déliverande
WN23a

Small shelter
Tobruk
Mortar Tobruk
U type Ringstand for a PzT FT-MG311(f) turret
Personnel shelters and stores
H666 bunker with 89P6 observation cupola
Open emplacement for artillery
Ringstand for 5cm antitank gun
H630 casemate for heavy MG
H612 casemate for a 7.5cm FK gun (moved from open emplacement)
SK Doppelschartenstand for 5cm gun
H677 casemate for 8.8cm anti-tank gun
H669 casemate for an 7.5cm FK16 gun
Anti-tank ditch

Canadian Scottish   **Royal Winnipeg Rifles**   **Regina Rifles**

C Coy

D Coy   B Coy   A Coy   B Coy

Château Vaux

La Valette

Courseulles-sur-Mer

0   500 yds
0   500 m

Opposite: *The defences of Juno Beach and, below, detail of the attack on Courseulles-sur-Mer. The coastal strongpoints (WN26–33a) were manned by companies of Grenadier-Regt 736 of the 716. Infanterie-Division with back-up units of Ost-Bataillon 441 at Reviers – Russians, who fought surprisingly well – and artillery (7./Artillerie-Regt 1716). The division had 7,771 men in total and about 1,500 of them were in strong bunkers and fortifications along Juno Beach.*

Left: *The North Shore Regt heads towards Nan Red. They had a tough fight around Saint-Aubin until the tanks of the Fort Garry Horse helped take out the German WN27 strongpoint. They then advanced to Douvres to attack the radar station (the Germans' codename for it was Stellung – position – 'Distelfink') which was manned by troops that had escaped inland from the coast as well as the radar station's crew of Luftwaffe technicians, the 8. Flugmelde-Leit-Kompanie of Luft-Nachrichten-Regt 53. The position was well-entrenched (it was four storeys deep) and heavily fortified and the Canadians, even with armour support, couldn't take it. In fact, it didn't surrender until a major attack on 16/17 June by No 41 Cdo – helped by 44 armoured vehicles and artillery support – used flail tanks to clear the minefields and AVREs to attack the casemates. The Germans – 227 of them – finally surrendered on 17 June.*

Below: *There aren't many photographs of the first moments of D-Day on the beaches of Normandy other than the famous sequence taken by Robert Capa on Omaha Beach. This photo was taken during Exercise Fabius and shows how it looked when there was no opposition emptying machine guns into the landing craft as the bow ramps dropped. The Germans had had many months to prepare for the invasion and select the position of their bunkers, heavy weapons, machine guns, barbed-wire entanglements, minefields and snipers. Indeed, it is surprising when one examines the defences that anyone lived to get off the beaches – 6 June saw 381 Canadian servicemen die with the total casualty figures over 1,000 (including wounded and captured).*

At the western end of Juno, opposite Graye-sur-Mer (**A**) and the Château de Vaux (**Below**), lay the beaches codenamed Mike Green and Red. There was a great deal of congestion as vehicles tried to get off these through two main gaps (see opposite): M2 to Graye (**D**) was blocked by a tank trap (**C**) and then a huge water-filled crater (**B**). It took some time (and the loss of an AVRE in the crater) to create a causeway but it wasn't working well until at least 12:00 on D-Day.

Above: *Vertical photo of the area after capture. Graye and the Château de Vaux are off the image at* **A** *and* **B** *respectively. The buried AVRE was at* **C**. **E** *is the location of the heavy MG bunker (see map p34).* **D** *shows the M2 exit from the beach and* **F** *the M1 exit. WN33 (**G**) is off the map to the west.*

Below: *This is 'One Charlie' the AVRE buried under the bridge at* **C**. *It was exhumed in 1976 and today stands nearby.*

Opposite: *Courseulles-sur-Mer showing the two exit lanes M2 (**A**) and M1(**B**). The two modern photos were taken at 1 (**Centre**) and 2 (**Below**). They show at **C** the 666 observation bunker with armoured cupola (also **Right**) and the Juno Beach Centre at **D**. The huge Croix de Lorraine (**E**) remembers Charles de Gaulle's return to France after four years of exile; at **F**, not quite visible above the bushes is the location for the AVRE on p35; **G** is the 630 casemate for heavy MG that formed the westerly edge of strongpoint WN31. The RWR came under heavy fire, arriving at around 07:50 ahead of their DD support. B Coy lost three-quarters of its men, but the regiment was still able to clear the beach and reach Creully, inland, by dusk.*

Above: *Details of the main weapons of WN31. There were also a number of Tobruks for MGs and mortars in the sand dunes and on the island. 1 The 5cm Doppelschartenstand could fire down both beaches; 2 (and **Right**) 666 bunker; 3 Tobruk with FT17 tank turret; 4 Vf69 Tobruk for mortar; 5 (and **Below**) 612 casemate for a 7.5cm FK gun – known as Cosy's bunker today after the commander of the attack on it, Lt W.A. 'Cosy' Aitken (note the Formstein concrete block construction); 6 location of an MG Vf58; 7 630 heavy MG bunker with Tobruk attached.*

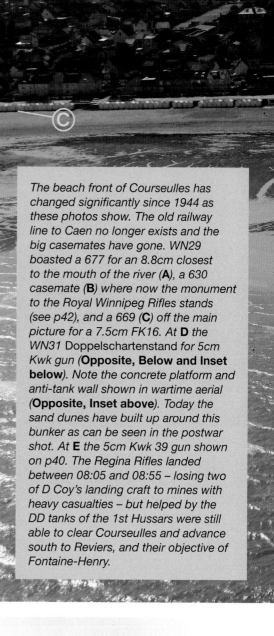

The beach front of Courseulles has changed significantly since 1944 as these photos show. The old railway line to Caen no longer exists and the big casemates have gone. WN29 boasted a 677 for an 8.8cm closest to the mouth of the river (**A**), a 630 casemate (**B**) where now the monument to the Royal Winnipeg Rifles stands (see p42), and a 669 (**C**) off the main picture for a 7.5cm FK16. At **D** the WN31 Doppelschartenstand for 5cm Kwk gun (**Opposite, Below and Inset below**). Note the concrete platform and anti-tank wall shown in wartime aerial (**Opposite, Inset above**). Today the sand dunes have built up around this bunker as can be seen in the postwar shot. At **E** the 5cm Kwk 39 gun shown on p40. The Regina Rifles landed between 08:05 and 08:55 – losing two of D Coy's landing craft to mines with heavy casualties – but helped by the DD tanks of the 1st Hussars were still able to clear Courseulles and advance south to Reviers, and their objective of Fontaine-Henry.

Right: *WN29 was concentrated around coastal frontage of Courseulles. This is the 677 bunker at the river mouth and its 8.8cm Pak 43/41. After D-Day it had a Canadian AA triple 20mm Polsten cannon on the roof above it. This casemate was probably put out of action by DD tanks of B Sqn, 1st Hussars, although the casemate bore signs of damage from shells fired by the destroyers and LCGs offshore.*

Below Right: *With the 677 to its right (**A**), this 5cm Kwk 39 in its Vf600 Ringstand was sited on the harbour wall. Today it has been moved a bit further back but the gun is the same.*

Opposite, Above Left: *After subduing WN29 the next step was WN30, set up in houses in the south of the city. Following this the Canadians advanced south. This Sherman DD of B Sqn, 1st Hussars is heading south down rue de l'Eglise towards Bény.*

Opposite, Above Right: *The 2nd Can Armd Bde supplied the DD tanks to support the landings – two squadrons of the 1st Hussars and two of the Fort Garry Horse. All told, 80 were embarked, those of the Fort Garry Horse disembarking straight onto the beach. 30 of 1st Hussars' tanks were launched at 1,000yd and 25 landed. The Centaurs of 2nd (RM) Assault Support Regt were the first SP artillery ashore and played an important part in destroying beach defences. This is one of 1st Hussars' DD M4A4 Shermans recovered from the seabed in 1970.*

Opposite, Below: *Another disabled DD Sherman of the 1st Hussars alongside a Crusader III AA Mk I gun in front of the 630 casemate at the top of Nan Green Beach (**C**). The Crusaders provided the initial light AA defence for the lodgement, towing an additional 40mm gun onto the beach, dropping it and its ammunition into a suitable location before moving to another. They were followed up with wheeled versions – Morris C9/Bs.*

Above and Below: *The monument to the Royal Winnipeg Rifles, of 7th Inf Bde stands where a bunker (C and also on p43) used to be. It and others in the town were knocked out by Sherman DDs. The first tanks on Nan Green Beach were B Sqn of the 1st Hussars – 14 reaching shore.*

Below: *Men of the Regina Rifles, 7th Inf Bde, follow a DD Sherman of B Sqn, 1st Hussars down rue de l'Eglise (today's rue Amiral Robert). The Reginas had 108 casualties on D-Day – as compared to the Royal Winnipeg Rifles' 128 – the Reginas landing on Nan Green and the 'Little Black Devils' on Mike Beach.*

Above: *Courseulles on D+1 as tanks head east along rue Emile Héroult in the direction of Bernières.*

Above Right: *M10s of 3rd Anti-Tank Regiment, RCA have their deep wading waterproofing removed after arriving over Mike Red Beach. This unit was the 3rd Can Inf Div's divisional anti-tank regiment, one of the first two deployed (the other was I Corps' 62nd Anti-Tank Regiment, RA). Between them they provided towed 6pdr and 17pdr guns as well as M10s armed with 3in and British*

17pdr guns (today called Wolverines and Achilles respectively). The 3rd's M10s were grouped together into 105th Composite Anti-Tank Battery, RCA; the 62nd's 245th and 248th Batteries each had three troops of four 17pdr-armed M10s. 248th Battery landed on D-Day in support of 7th Inf Bde; 245th didn't arrive until D+2.

Below: *M10 in Bernières heading east on rue Berthélémy. It was vital that anti-tank regiments were in place quickly to face the anticipated German armoured counter-attacks.*

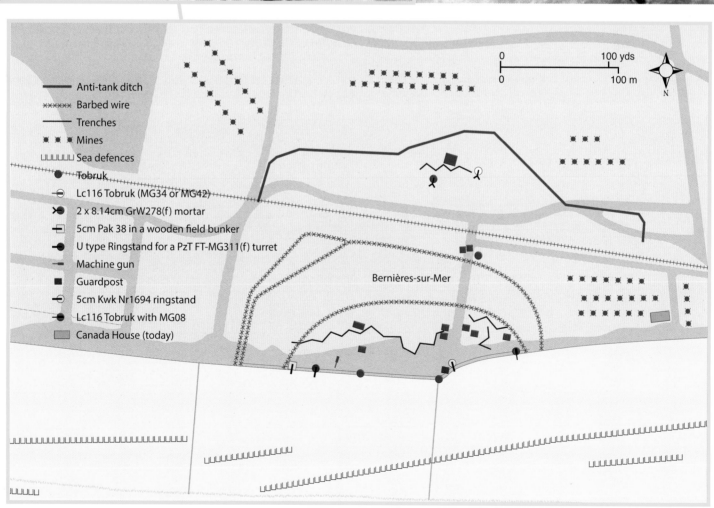

━━━	Anti-tank ditch
xxxxxx	Barbed wire
──	Trenches
■ ■ ■	Mines
∐∐∐∐	Sea defences
●	Tobruk
⊖	Lc116 Tobruk (MG34 or MG42)
✗	2 x 8.14cm GrW278(f) mortar
⊟	5cm Pak 38 in a wooden field bunker
⊷	U type Ringstand for a PzT FT-MG311(f) turret
━	Machine gun
■	Guardpost
⊖	5cm Kwk Nr1694 ringstand
⊷	Lc116 Tobruk with MG08
▬	Canada House (today)

Bernières-sur-Mer

0   100 yds
0   100 m

N

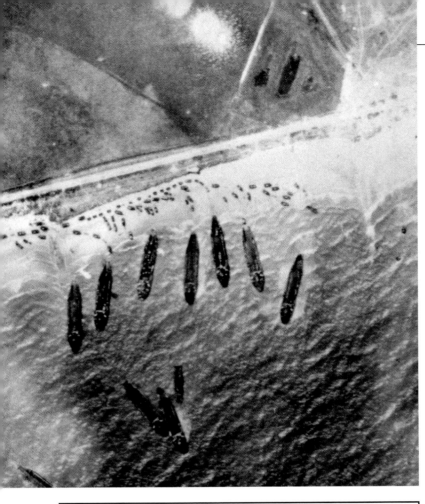

Bernières-sur-Mer – Nan White – was a mile east of Courseulles and was the target of the Queen's Own Rifles of Canada of 8th Inf Bde. B Coy landed in front of WN28 where there was a tall sea wall, and lost 65 men. The DD tanks of the Fort Garry Horse were landed after the infantry. The strongpoint was crossed by a railway line (no longer there) and contained by an anti-tank wall, barbed wire and a minefield. It had a range of heavy weapons.

*Key to photo (**Above Right**):*

1 *A 5cm Pak 38 in a wooden field bunker was here.*
2 and Right *Canada Place with its 5cm Kwk gun in a Nr1694-type Ringstand.*
3 and Above *Ic116 Tobruk with MG08 machine gun.*
4 *Location of today's Canada House (see also p47).*
T *Tobruks.*

Above: *An LCT loaded with Shermans of 2nd Can Armd Bde sails along the coast off Bernières-sur-Mer. Note the barrage balloons, intended to discourage low-level attacks by German aircraft. They were towed by some of the larger assault vessels.*

Below: *Maj Gen Rod Keller (**A**) and some of his staff come ashore on Nan White Beach at Bernières at 11:45 on the morning of D-Day. They wear a variety of interesting uniforms. The man on the left wears a leather jerkin, dispatch rider's helmet and goggles. The man behind wears the short-lived and unpopular assault jerkin, an early attempt to make a single-piece accoutrement to hold all a man's equipment rather than a webbing set made up of separate straps*

*and components. The officer on Keller's left is Brig R.A. Wyman (**B**), commanding 2nd Can Armd Bde (note shoulder insignia – a black lozenge with a blue stripe). He has a pair of Canadian-produced binoculars which had a distinctly different shape to the standard British prismatic binoculars carried by his compatriots. This man, and the two behind him, wear the Mk III helmet which had a turtle shape and offered greater protection than the traditional soup-bowl-shaped helmet that had been in use since World War I. Keller wears a beret with a general's badge. He was a dynamic leader known for his trenchant language, but by the time he was wounded by friendly fire on 8 August (US bombers) his command was on borrowed time as he was showing signs of stress.*

This Page: *One of the best-remembered landmarks in Bernières, today it's called Canada House (**A**). Note the SBG assault bridge (**B**) in place on the seawall. The photo was taken around midday on 6 June as the Stormont, Dundas and Glengarry Highlanders, part of the reserve 9th Inf Bde, came ashore. Note the spire of Notre-Dame-de-la-Nativité, seen (**Below**) on the afternoon of 6 June as more follow-up troops cross Nan White. Canada House was liberated by the Queen's Own Rifles of Canada, but at the cost of over 100 casualties. With 9th Bde came the Shermans of the Sherbrooke Fusilier Regt of 2nd Can Armd Bde. They were tasked with exploiting the bridgehead and advancing towards Carpiquet airfield. They advanced with the North Nova Scotia Highlanders*

Right and Below: *Nan Red at La Rive, just to the west of Saint-Aubin-sur-Mer, is where the North Shore Regt landed at around 08:00. Many years ago, in their classic book on the D-Day landings, the* After the Battle *team identified the location of the house shown in the film from which this still was taken (identified by the* **arrow** *on the photograph). The mass of craters were created by a salvo of LCR rockets. Today, the house in question – named* Les Hirondelles, *the Swallows – has a photographic board outside.*

Bottom: *All that remains of WN27 – a covered Ringstand with a 5cm gun at the top of rue Gustave Canet. It can also be seen at* **A** *opposite. It was knocked out by tank fire.*

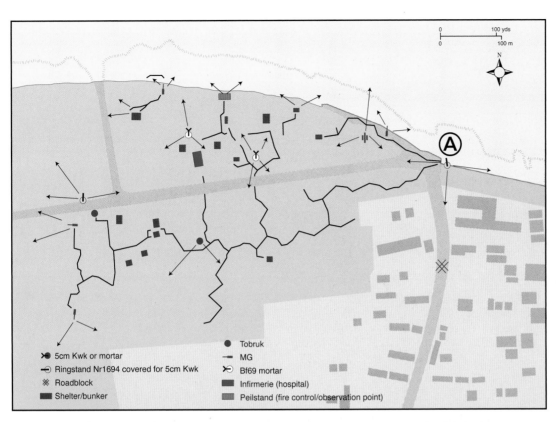

Scale: 0 — 100 yds / 0 — 100 m

N

Ⓐ

Legend:
- ✕— 5cm Kwk or mortar
- ⊖ Ringstand Nr1694 covered for 5cm Kwk
- ✳ Roadblock
- ▪ Shelter/bunker
- ● Tobruk
- — MG
- ✕— Bf69 mortar
- ▬ Infirmerie (hospital)
- ▬ Peilstand (fire control/observation point)

This Page: *Saint-Aubin-sur-Mer's defences were concentrated around WN27. The Germans cleared houses and introduced barbed wire, minefields and defensive points interlinked by a trench system that held up the attackers. No 48 Cdo landed under the guns of WN27 (they were tasked with clearing beach defences to the east and linking up with No 41 Cdo who were to have done the same westward from Sword Beach). Neither force was strong enough to subdue the opposition quickly, and No 48 Cdo sustained high casualties (over 100 dead) on the beach.* **B** *identifies a house with a 2cm Flak on top;* **C** *= roadblock (see p50). The Peilstand was for observation and fire control of 7./Artillerie-Regt 1716's four guns at WN28a (see map p32).*

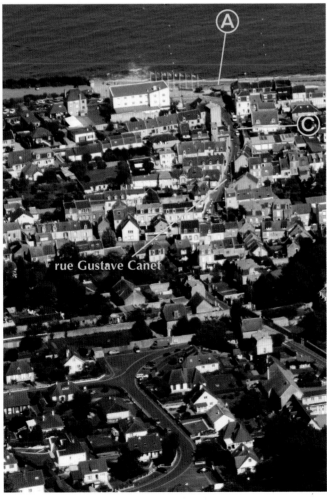

rue Gustave Canet

Ⓐ

Ⓒ

Ⓒ

Ⓐ

Ⓑ

Opposite, Above and Center: *Very little remains of the sea wall to the west of Saint-Aubin. As the tide came in, there wasn't much space for the attacking forces, pinned down by the strongpoints.*

Opposite, Below: *The roadblock on rue Canet, with the 5cm bunker at* **A***. It was taken out by a DD Sherman. The men are either from the North Shore Regt or commandos from No 4 Special Service Bde.*

Above and Centre Right: *Saint-Aubin as seen from the WN27 5cm Ringstand. On the beach can be seen a P-47 Thunderbolt and a Fort Garry Horse DD Sherman. The North Shore Regt and No 48 Cdo landed here (Nan Red) and suffered badly after an ineffective pre-landing bombardment. The 5cm was finally put out of action by tank and AVRE fire, but by that time 48 Cdo had lost nearly half its men. On 10 June, the P-47D of 2Lt John A. Weese of 386th FS, 365th FG was hit and belly-landed on the beach. Unfortunately, Weese died of his wounds.*

Below and Bottom: *The town beach at Saint-Aubin has high walls which made leaving it difficult – which is why the main landings were to the west.* **A** *identifies the 5cm Ringstand,* **B** *the hillock where the main defensive area of WN27 was centred and where the Romans had built a fort. It dominated the beach. The houses in Saint-Aubin to left and right of WN27 were linked, strengthened and defended which accounts for the fires raging as the North Shore Regt cleaned them out.*

Inukshuk

Empilement de pierres formant un point de repère, représentant ici un modèle humain comme en construisent les Inuit dans l'Arctique Canadien. Il symbolise la fraternité, le respect mutuel et l'amitié entre les peuples

Inukshuk

A piling of stones forming a landmark representing here a human as constructed by the Inuit in the Canadian Arctic. It symbolises brotherhood, mutual respect and friendship between peoples.

The inukshuk *is a crude figure made of piled stones. It has become a symbol of Canada and can be found today in a number of places in Normandy where Canadians fought. These three are from:*
- *Juno Beach, near Canada House, Bernières-sur-Mer (Top Left)*
- *the Juno Beach Centre at Courseulles-sur-Mer (Top Right)*
- *remembering the Queen's Own Rifles of Canada at Anguerny (Left and Above).*

LOCATIONS OF INTEREST AROUND JUNO BEACH AREA

1   WN33A bunker on coast outside Graye-sur-Mer.
2   Inns of Court Monument to men of 11th (BR) Armd Div.
3   Plaques remembering the Royal Winnipeg Rifles and the 1st Canadian Scottish.
4   'One Charlie' Churchill AVRE (p35).
5   One of 10 Signal memorials erected at key landing sites.
6   Monument to 1st (Pol) Armd Div.
7   Croix de Lorraine where de Gaulle landed (p36).
8   'Cosy's bunker' – a 612 casemate for an 7.5cm FK gun (p37).
9   A well-preserved Vf69 mortar Tobruk.
10 Nottingham Bridge over the Seulle.
11 Monument to the Royal Canadian Navy.
12 Restored 666 observation bunker.
13 *Inukshuk* – see **Opposite, Above Right**.
14 Juno Beach Centre (p36).
15 German Grenadier-Regt 736 underground command bunker.

16 Recently restored 1c116 MG Tobruk.
17 Doppelschartenstand 5cm bunker (p39).
18 50mm Kwk 39 gun (p40).
19 1st Hussars' M4A4 Sherman DD (p41).
20 Memorial to 1st Can Scottish Regt, 8th Bn, the Royal Scots Fusiliers, 6th Border Bn, KOSB and 44th (Lowland) Inf Bde.
21 Memorial to *La Combattante*, the ship that carried de Gaulle (sank 1945).
22 War Memorial.
23 Monument to the Regina Rifles Regt, 22nd Dragoons and RE Inland Waterways Transportation Companies.
24 Monument to the RWR (p42).
25 Canada House (p47) – also plaque to the Queen's Own Rifles of Canada.
26 *Inukshuk* – see **Opposite, Above Left**.
27 Ernest W. Parker stain-glass window in church.
28 War memorial outside church.
29 Monument to the Fort Garry Horse.
30 Monument to the Régiment de la Chaudière.

31 Monument to Canadian troops.
32 Canada Place – bunker and memorials to the Stormont, Dundas and Glengarry Highlanders, Queen's Own Rifles of Canada, 22nd Dragoons, and the Royal Berkshire Regt (p45).
33 Canadian bikes sculpture.
34 Monument to the 14th Field Regt, RCA.
35 Monument to the North Shore Regt.
36 WN27 gun emplacement, Saint-Aubin-sur-Mer (pp48–49).
37 Fort Garry Horse monument.
38 Museum of Radar and defensive positions outside Douvres la Délivrande.
39 Canadian War cemetery in Bény-sur-Mer (p159).
40 Memorial to Regina Rifle Regt in Reviers (p65).
41 Just off map, Canadian liberation memorial at Basly (p65).
42 **(inset)** Memorial to the Queen's Own Rifles of Canada at Anisy (south of Basly).

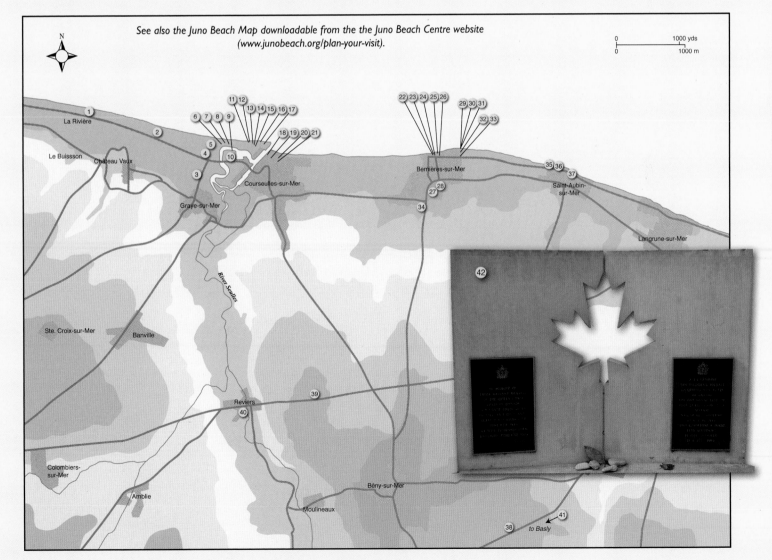

See also the Juno Beach Map downloadable from the the Juno Beach Centre website
(www.junobeach.org/plan-your-visit).

Left: *The photographs of soldiers clutching bicycles making their way down the gangways of landing ships (see p27) highlight one of the D-Day plans that had definitely mixed success. Unlike the Japanese 'bicycle Blitzkrieg' in Malaya, the use of pushbikes in Normandy doesn't seem to have worked particularly well and many of them – to the delight of the locals – were quickly abandoned, although there were still some in evidence crossing the Seine or to be seen as tank crew runabouts in the Netherlands and Germany. The BSA folding bike, originally developed for use by Airborne troops, was the main type used. One company in each of D-Day's follow-up battalions were to use them to keep up if the advances outpaced the footsloggers.*

Above Right: *The Canadian Beach Commandos trained in Scotland and at Exbury on the Solent. They played an important role supervising beach clearance, landings and evacuation of wounded etc. Here men of RCN Beach Commando 'W' landing on Mike Beach on 8 July relieving 'P' Commando. Note the 'turtle' Mk III helmets.*

Centre Right: *Once the Mulberry Harbours were in place, troops could be more easily landed – as here.*

Right: *The invaders needed to maintain the supply of material during the Normandy campaign, and many cargo vessels were used to achieve this – such as Yokefleet, an 822-ton cargo ship launched in 1910, seen standing off Courseulles-sur-Mer unloading into waiting DUKW amphibious trucks. The Channel ports were unable to carry the levels of supplies hoped for, but the operations over the beaches of Utah and Omaha more than made up for this.*

1st Canadian Parachute Battalion

Championed by Col (later Lt Gen) E.L.M. Burns, the history of Canadian paratroops started officially on 1 July 1942 when the Department of National Defence authorised the formation of a battalion (a second became part of the short-lived American-Canadian First Special Service Force). Training at both Fort Benning and in England, the unit ended up in the UK under the command of Lt Col G.F.P. Bradbrooke as part of 3rd Para Bde, 6th (BR) Airborne Division.

Earmarked for direct involvement in Operation Overlord, 6th Airborne's mission was part of Operation Tonga, the codename for British and Canadian paratroop and glider-borne operations on the night of 5/6 June. 6th Airborne was tasked with protecting the eastern flank of the Allied seaborne landings with three main tasks: to capture intact the two bridges at Bénouville (today they are called Pegasus and Horsa); to knock out the Merville coastal artillery battery and to destroy a number of bridges over the Rivers Dives and Divette.

By cutting off access to the bridges over the Orne and Canal de Caen, 6th Airborne effectively sealed off the eastern flank of the Allied beachhead. By keeping them intact, they could be used to reinforce the airborne troops. The attack on the Merville Battery had a more straightforward reason: it was well-placed to shell Sword Beach and the plan was to stop this from happening. The small bridges over the Dives and Divette ensured that the few dry causeways over the flooded marshlands of the area were closed to a quick German response to the invasion.

1st Can Para Bn's part in this was:
- *A Company* (Maj D. Wilkins) to cover 9th Para Bn's left flank in its approach march and attack on Merville Battery and then advanced to Le Plain. After this, it – and the rest of the battalion – would take and hold the key strategic crossroads at Le Mesnil.
- *B Company* (Maj C. Fuller) with a section of 3rd Para Sqn, RE under command had to destroy the bridges over the River

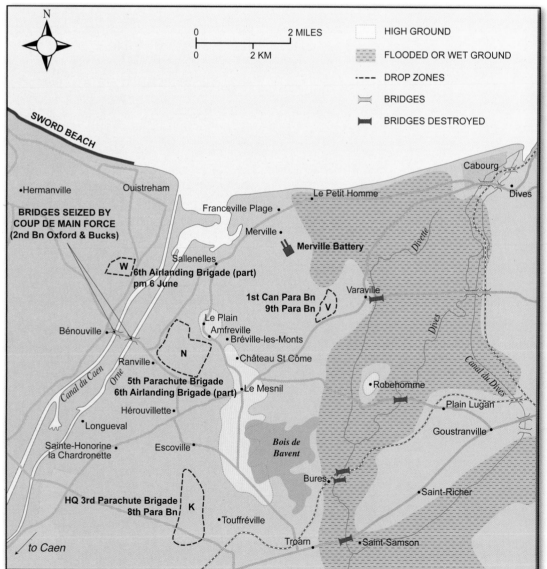

Map key:
- HIGH GROUND
- FLOODED OR WET GROUND
- ---- DROP ZONES
- BRIDGES
- BRIDGES DESTROYED

Left: *Operation Tonga and 6th Airborne Div's battleground east of the Orne*

Below: *Canadian memorial at Varaville remembers the fighting by 9th Para Bn and 1st Can Para Bn on 6 June.*

Above: *Lt Col G.F.P. Bradbrooke, CO 1st Can Para Bn (left), and his deputy, Maj Jeff A. Nicklin, outside Battalion HQ, Carter Barracks, Bulford, January 1944. They are wearing battledress with a pair of Canadian jump wings sewn to the left breast, a distinctive insignia unique to Canada featuring a maple leaf beneath a parachute with a pair of stylised wings to either side. Nicklin, who died during Operation Varsity, took over as CO from Bradbrooke's temporary successor, Maj G.F. Eadie.*

Above Right: *Brig S. James L. Hill (right) was the inspirational commander of the 3rd Para Bde. By the end of the war he had amassed the DSO and two bars, MC and American Silver Star not to mention the French Legion d'Honneur. Here he briefs officers of the 1st Can Para Bn at Bulford, 6 December 1943, L–R: Cap R.A. MacDonald, Maj P.R. Griffin, unidentified British officer, Maj Jeff A. Nicklin, Hill.*

Centre Right: *Carter Barracks, Bulford again, a gathering of senior NCOs, L–R RSM 'Knobby' Clark, Company Sgt Norbert Joseph and CSM Outhwaite – of 1st Can Para Bn, just prior to the unit leaving for the transit camp before D-Day. Note the gold-yellow loops around the base of the battledress shoulder straps. These distinguished the Canadian Paras within the British 3rd Para Bde. Canadian parachute troops wore the same camouflaged cotton Denison over-smock as the British and Polish parachute troops landing on D-Day. The officer on the left has slung a Sten bandolier over his webbing. This accoutrement allowed a man to carry an extra seven magazines for his sub-machine gun. Note, too, the Paratroop helmets and the rank insignia visible on the lower right sleeves – WOI's British Royal Arms (the change to Canadian took place after the war) and WOII (centre).*

Right: *Paras of the 1st Can Para Bn in a transit camp staging area prior to D-Day, c1–5 June 1944.*

Above, Centre and Below Left: *The bridge at Robehomme that was blown by the Canadians. The modern view shows that it might not be particularly wide, but it is a substantial obstacle for vehicles.*

Above: *The bridge over the Divette at Varaville. A plaque on it remembers its destruction by 3rd Para Sqn, RE and 1st Can Para Bn.*

Opposite: *Le Mesnil crossroads sits astride a strategically important junction giving access to the Bavent ridge which gave views over the left flank of the Allied seaborne invasion – a good reason to hold the position and deny its vantage point to the Germans. There were strong elements of the German 21. Panzer-Division in the area and these were a threat on D-Day, but never approached the crossroads. The German counter-attacks would come over the following days, but the Canadians held the position, destroying several tanks in the process. At **A** the brickworks where the battalion mortars were set up. On 12 June Battalion HQ moved position from around the château (**B**) to the brickworks. After its period out of the line (17–24 June) the battalion moved back to Le Mesnil and the HQ was set up again in the brickworks.*

Dives at Robehomme and then hold the feature (Robehomme is on a hillock) until ordered to withdraw to Le Mesnil crossroads.

- *C Company* (Maj H.M. MacLeod) was to secure DZ-V, destroy an enemy signal exchange and positions at Varaville, then blow the bridge over the Divette before it, too, joined the rest of the battalion at the crossroads.

The problem was that – for a variety of reasons: Flak, weather, navigation and beacon problems – the paratroops were scattered on delivery and often had to complete their tasks with insufficient men and equipment. While 6th Airborne performed brilliantly, completing all its missions and making light of the delivery problems, they weren't able to knock out the Merville Battery completely and the Germans were able to bring two guns back into action.

Elsewhere, the bridges at Bénouville were taken; those over the Dives and the Divette blown; Varaville was taken and held until relieved by British Commandos (many of whom arrived on bicycles). The elements of the battalion then moved separately to the crossroads at Le Mesnil – where the Bn HQ had been since 11:00 on 6 June – the last elements of B Coy arriving at 02:30 on 8 June. The *Battalion War Diary* records a German counter-attack by Grenadier-Regts 857 and 858 supported by SP guns and PzKpfw IVs on the 7th. It was broken up by mortar fire. The position was held until the battalion was moved to a rest area on 17 June.

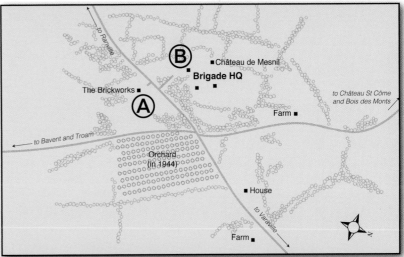

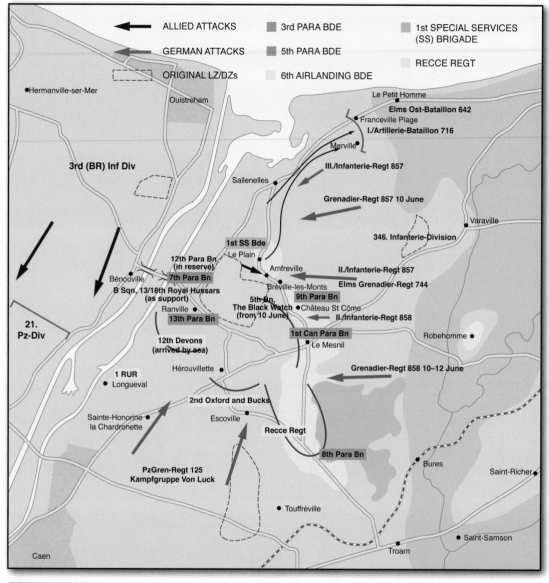

Map legend:
- ALLIED ATTACKS
- GERMAN ATTACKS
- ORIGINAL LZ/DZs
- 3rd PARA BDE
- 5th PARA BDE
- 6th AIRLANDING BDE
- 1st SPECIAL SERVICES (SS) BRIGADE
- RECCE REGT

Map labels:
Hermanville-ser-Mer • Ouistreham • Le Petit Homme • Elms Ost-Bataillon 642 • Franceville Plage • I./Artillerie-Bataillon 716 • Merville • III./Infanterie-Regt 857 • Sallenelles • 3rd (BR) Inf Div • Grenadier-Regt 857 10 June • Varaville • 1st SS Bde • Le Plain • 346. Infanterie-Division • 12th Para Bn (in reserve) • 7th Para Bn • Amfreville • II./Infanterie-Regt 857 • Bénouville • B Sqn, 13/18th Royal Hussars (as support) • Bréville-les-Monts • Elms Grenadier-Regt 744 • 5th Bn, The Black Watch (from 10 June) • 9th Para Bn • Château St Côme • Ranville • 13th Para Bn • II./Infanterie-Regt 858 • 1st Can Para Bn • Le Mesnil • Robehomme • 21. Pz-Div • 12th Devons (arrived by sea) • Hérouvillette • Grenadier-Regt 858 10–12 June • 1 RUR • Longueval • 2nd Oxford and Bucks • Sainte-Honorine la Chardronette • Escoville • Recce Regt • 8th Para Bn • Bures • Saint-Richer • PzGren-Regt 125 Kampfgruppe Von Luck • Touffréville • Saint-Samson • Troarn • Caen

Left: *The German attacks on 6th Airborne, 10–12 June. A strong force of Germans occupied Château de Côme on 10 June and used it as a base to start an infantry and SP gun assault on the British. The next German attack used II./Grenadier-Regt 857, I. and II./Grenadier-Regt 858 and several companies of Grenadier-Regt 744: it took hand-to-hand fighting to beat them off. The rest of the German assault came up against the 1st Can Para Bn, and was stopped by an artillery bombardment. Two later attacks suffered the same fate. Later at 23:00 C Coy, 9th Para Bn fought its way to and occupied the château, and fought off several small attacks throughout the night. On the 11th, reinforcements came in the form of the British 51st (Highland) Div when a company of 5th Bn, Black Watch took over the defence of the château. Heavy fighting ensued and only ceased when Bréville was attacked and taken. A statue of a Black Watch piper and the memorial of the battle (**Below Left**) sit outside the château.*

Below: *21st Army Group commander Gen Bernard Montgomery presents Capt John Hanson, C Coy, 1st Can Para Bn with the MC, on 16 July 1944. C Coy had been tasked with clearing the enemy from Varaville, destroying a radio transmitter station and blowing the bridge over the Divette. Hanson was 2IC but after Company CO Maj Murray McLeod was killed early in the fighting, Hanson and the few men at his disposal took and held the enemy position – complete with 7.5cm gun – until relieved by Commandos from Sword Beach. During the fighting they heard an enormous explosion – the bridge going up! – and not too long after the Germans surrendered. Hanson's leadership and valour led to the award of an MC.*

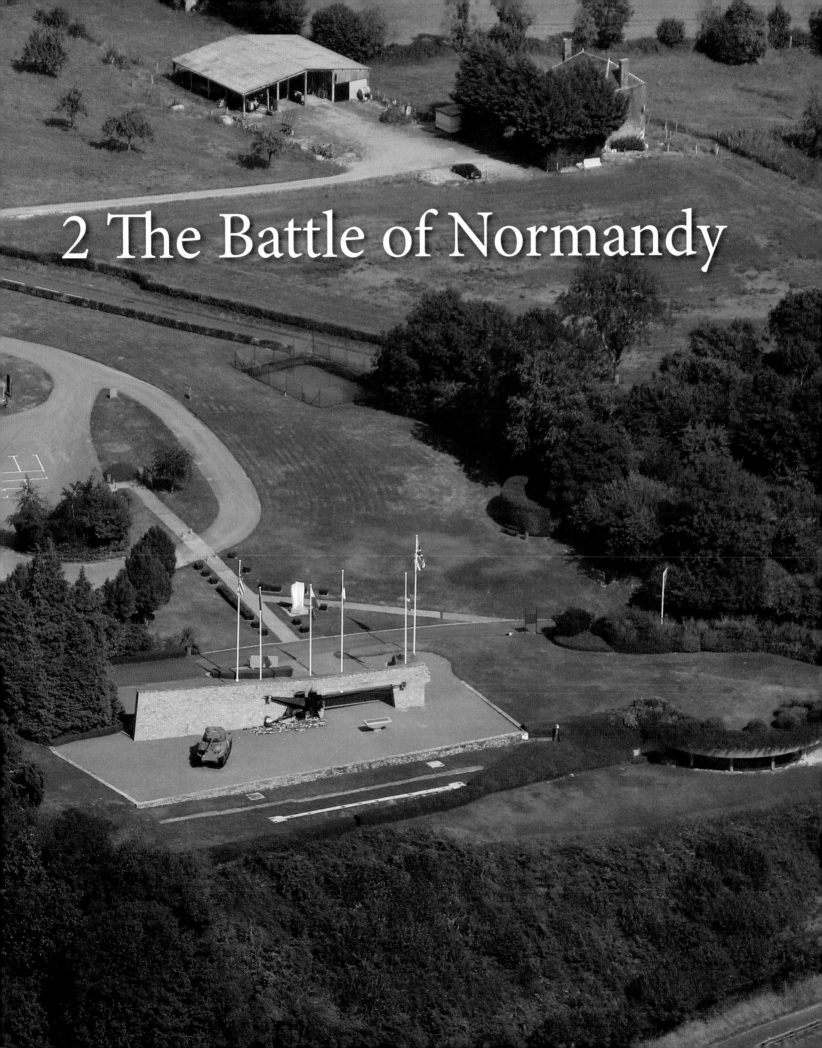

2 The Battle of Normandy

Canadian troops played an important role in the battle of Normandy, contributing materially to the Allies' massive victory. They were there at the beginning, having landed on D-Day when they pressed inland farther than any other units, if not smashing their objectives then certainly getting close. They then withstood the immediate counter-attacks benefitting from the assistance their mobile SP artillery could bring, and starting a duel with the 12.SS-Panzer-Division *Hitlerjugend* that got very personal. Over 150 Canadians would be murdered in cold blood by the Germans and a postwar trial saw their commander, SS-Standartenführer Kurt 'Panzer' Meyer, found guilty of war crimes.

Meyer was a self-serving Nazi fanatic and for too long too much credence has been given to him and his fellow travellers who sought to play up the strength of the German soldier's tactics and weaponry at the expense of the Allies. In fact the Allies gave as good as they got, and the scenes of death and destruction around St-Lambert-sur-Dive and Chambois were an awful reckoning. Fighting in a country they had held for four years, in terrain that benefitted the defender, the Germans used threats to ensure that their men held fast: over 40,000 were executed during the war.

During the three-month long battle the Canadian presence in Normandy grew from an infantry division with tank support to a full army, and while a sizeable proportion of its units weren't Canadian but British or Polish, they still fought under the same command – the training, equipment, clothing and armaments coming from a common base. Overhead, they were supported by Allied air forces, many of those from 2TAF coming from the RCAF squadrons of No 83 Group.

First Canadian Army showed time after time that it had more than a stomach for the fight, grinding out the hard yards around Caen while learning the ropes – experience that would stand them in good stead in the battles to come. While their losses were great – the Canadian butcher's bill for Normandy was nearly 19,000 with over 5,000 dead – those of their enemy was even worse. The Germans sustained 210,000 casualties in the campaign, a figure that increases to well over 400,000 including those captured.

Today, there are memorials aplenty to see all over Normandy from Courseulles-sur-Mer to St-Lambert and there's no doubt that walking battlefields gives insights into why events progressed as they did: the constrained hedgerows of the bocage are still in evidence as is the more tank-friendly countryside south of Caen. And, sometimes surprisingly considering it has been over 70 years, there are many places that look the same as they did then, allowing direct comparisons. *After the Battle*'s epic two-volume study of D-Day and follow-up on the *Rückmarsch* (the German retreat) are well-worth examining.

Previous Page: *The Mémorial de Montormel and museum sit atop Hill 262 (see p87).*

Below: *Men of Le Régiment de la Chaudière, 8th Inf Bde, head off the beaches towards Bény-sur-Mer. Today there is a major Canadian cemetery there (see p156–157).*

Above: *Memorial to the 24 men of the Royal Winnipeg Rifles and two Green Howards who were murdered in the grounds of the Château d'Andrieu on the night of 7/8 June 1944.*

Above Right: *Authie has particular connotations for Canada. Taken on 7 June by the North Nova Scotia Highlanders supported by the Sherbrooke Fusilier Regt who were advancing towards Carpiquet airfield, it was retaken after hand-to-hand fighting by SS-Pz-Regt 25 of the 12.SS-Pz-Div* Hitlerjugend. *The Germans then held it for another month. After the battle 23 Canadian prisoners – including three from the Sherbrooke Fusilier Regt – were executed by their* Hitlerjugend *captors. Today a memorial in Ardenne Abbey remembers the event. It would not be the last: troops of* Hitlerjugend *murdered as many as 156 Canadians in the following weeks.*

Centre Right: *L–R GFM Gerd von Rundstedt, SS-Standartenführer Kurt Meyer, SS-Obergruppenführer Josef Dietrich and SS-Oberführer Fritz Witt watching a* Hitlerjugend *drill. SS-Brigadeführer Franz Witt commanded* Hitlerjugend *but was killed on 14 June. Kurt Meyer took over. He had a history of war crimes in Russia and his men would continue in the same vein.*

Right: *Ardenne Abbey just outside Authie. Over 20 Canadians were murdered in the grounds 7–17 June.*

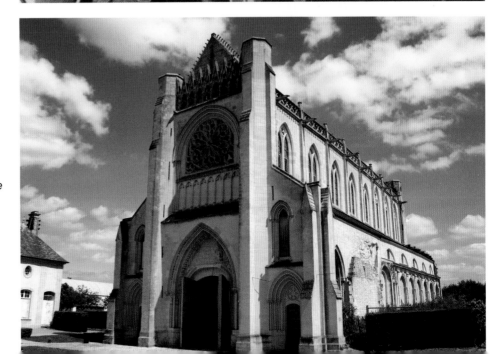

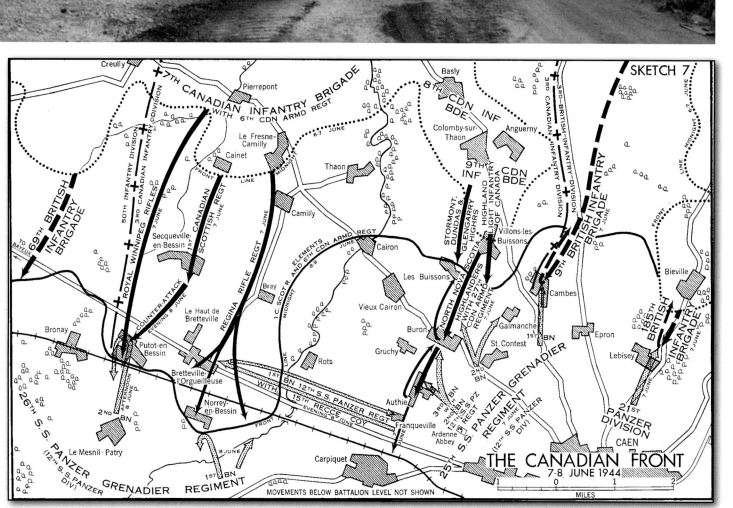

SKETCH 7

THE CANADIAN FRONT
7-8 JUNE 1944

MOVEMENTS BELOW BATTALION LEVEL NOT SHOWN

Opposite, Above: *Moving inland from the beaches, the Reginas advanced to Reviers where they concentrated before moving further south. The village folk remembered their liberation by erecting this memorial (**Right**).*

Opposite, Below: *After breaking through the coastal crust, the Canadian troops advanced steadily until digging in for the night. They continued their advance the next morning taking Authie and Buron, but were counter-attacked by Hitlerjugend who pushed them out of the two villages. On 7–8 June the fighting intensified as the Canadians tried to force their way south. The key day was 11 June when Rots was taken but the Canadians were savaged at Le Mesnil-Patry, losing 37 tanks and were forced to retreat.*

Left: *Many of the French villages remember their liberators. This is in Basly.*

Below: *The violent battle of Rots on 11 June was led by No 46 Cdo supported by the Chaudières and the Fort Garry Horse – one of whose Shermans is seen here alongside a jeep ambulance. It was knocked out by a Panther of SS-Pz-Regt 12. Hitlerjugend defended the area fanatically but were forced out with artillery help. The Fort Garry Horse lost 16 tanks.*

BASLY

EN HOMMAGE
ET RECONNAISSANCE AUX
LIBERATEURS CANADIENS
LE 6 JUIN 1944

RECOLLECTION
AND GRATITUDE TO THE
CANADIAN LIBERATORS
THE 6 JUNE 1944

BASLY LE 8 JUIN 1991

THE BATTLE OF BRETTEVILLE L'ORGUEILLEUSE

We often read of the superiority of German battle tactics. Allied tactics and fighting doctrine – and especially, its armour – all come off decidedly second best in comparison. This accusation is difficult to sustain when one examines this battle. As Marc Milner makes clear in his 2007 article 'The Guns of Bretteville', the German armoured counter-attacks were stymied by stern Anglo-Canadian defence that made use of all arms, but particularly, in the case of this battle, the mobile SP artillery of 13th Field Regt, RCA that had been landed on D-Day. The attack by the 21. Panzer-Division that reached the sea at Lion-sur-Mer on D-Day had been fired on by British guns on the Périers Ridge, where well-sited infantry anti-tank units of the Shropshire Light Infantry and Shermans of the Staffordshire Regiment had stopped one side of the attack dead in its tracks. Gen Edgar Feuchtinger, commander of 21. Panzer-Division, was more honest than SS-Standartenführer Kurt Meyer when he blamed the excellence of the Allied anti-tank guns rather than lack of petrol for the way that the German attacks on the Canadians were halted.

The first, powerful attacks on the 7th Brigade's positions by SS-PzGr-Regt 26 took place in daylight on the 8th, but they were quite easily negated by the artillery. This was down to careful preparatory work done on 7 June by the artillery and the infantry: some 33 targets had been prepared – for defensive fire (likely enemy forming up areas or approach routes); SOS tasks (to cover areas that defending infantry could not hit); or 'Mike' targets, which were calls for regimental shoots ('Uncle' called for a divisional shoot). Nearby, the Royal Winnipeg Rifles were pushed out of Putot but the village was retaken by the Canadian Scottish who were 'walked in' with artillery covering fire.

Meyer, commander of *Hitlerjugend*'s SS-PzGr-Regt 25, led the next attack on Bretteville on the night of 8/9 June. Spearheaded by PzKpfw V Panthers of two companies of 1./SS-Panzer-Regt 12 commanded by SS-Standartenführer Max Wünsche, it also included a battery of SP guns, Meyer expected that the Panzergrenadiers of SS-PzGr-Regt 26 would join in: they didn't thanks to the ministrations of 79th Med Regt, RA around Thaon.

The 3rd Anti-Tank Regt, RCA knocked out three of the attacking tanks on the outskirts of the village, forcing the others to withdraw. The two that did get in, around 12:00, were hunted down by PIAT teams. The biggest problem the defenders had was when wire from the FOOs back to the guns was cut.

This happened to one of the outlying defence points – Cardonville Farm – whose defenders were in a desperate position until they finally made radio contact and called down a bombardment as the Panzergrenadiers moved in. 'The accuracy,' Milner records Maj G. Brown saying, 'of the shelling was unbelievable ... nothing ever impressed me as much as [that] at Cardonville.' The German attack melted away.

At 13:00 on the 9th, Panzer Meyer put in his final attack: 3./SS-Panzer-Regt 12 headed towards Norrey-en-Bessin, a few miles to the south, which was defended by C Coy of the Reginas. The *Hitlerjugend* Panthers were ambushed by Shermans of 1st Hussars. Seven of them were destroyed in quick time, five of them by Lt G. K. Henry and his gunner Tpr A. Chapman, SS-PzGr-Regt 26 being kept at bay by the artillery.

Milner concluded that the training and doctrine worked superbly. Artillery stripped away the enemy infantry or prevented them from moving, leaving their tanks vulnerable.

Opposite, Left: *Another PzKpfw V from SS-Pz-Regt 12 destroyed in the German attack on Bretteville-l'Orgueilleuse. This one was knocked out on the road to the south of the town by anti-tank fire – probably a PIAT – and was rolled off the road by engineers to clear the way. The myth that more Panthers were lost because of automotive problems rather than battle damage, and that German tank-infantry tactics were pre-eminent on the Normandy battlefield, are exposed as unreliable in Gullachsen's 2016 examination of I./SS-Panzer-Regiment 12. Apart from the significant battle damage inflicted by Allied anti-tank units, he goes on to identify two major advantages of the Allies, even in the small lodgement area they had under control: their excellent repair and replacement facilities. Part of this was down to the availability of new equipment, part to the excellence of the Canadian replacement system by the 25th Can Armd Delivery Regt (the Elgin Regt). What it added up to was better serviceability and availability of tanks than the Germans.*

Opposite, Right: *Four RCA field regiments – 12th, 13th, 14th and 19th – landed on D-Day, providing 240 Priest SP 105mm guns such as this one from the 19th. Charge-seven gave them a max range of 12,500yd, but direct support ranges were much less than this.*

Above: *The Hitlerjugend PzKpfw V Ausf G was knocked out by a PIAT team of Riflemen Joseph E. LaPointe and Gill A. Carnie and L/Cpl Clarence V. Hewitt close to the Regina's HQ.*

Below Left: *A memorial in Bretteville-l'Orgueilleuse to the liberation of villages in the area from Le Fresne on the 6 June to Gruchy on 8 July.*

Below Right: *SS-Brigadeführer Kurt Meyer in court with escorts Maj Arthur Russel (left) and Capt Elton D. McPhail (right) at his trial for war crimes. Guilty and sentenced to death, the verdict was controversially commuted to life imprisonment. He served five years.*

Above Left: *Taking a chance to recover while they can, these are infantrymen of 9th Can Inf Bde resting in the Normandy bridgehead, 8–9 June 1944.*

Above Right: *Capt W. Noble of the Highland Light Infantry of Canada has found some straw to aid his slumbers. Note Sykes-Fairbairn Commando knife, Mk III 'turtle' helmet and Sten Mk III, 20 June.*

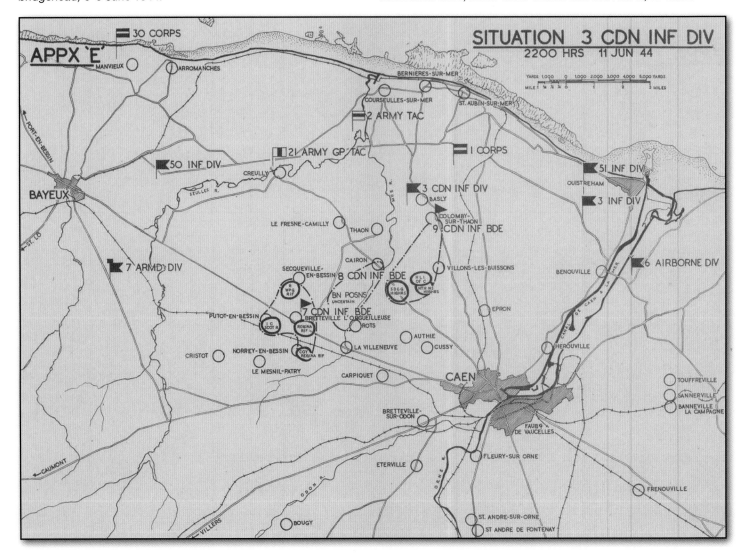

Above: *3rd Can Inf Div's most senior officers on 25 June. Front row: (from second left to right) Brig R.A. Wyman (OC 2nd Can Armd Bde), Brig H.W. Foster (OC 7th Inf Bde, later GOC 4th Can Armd Div), Maj Gen R.F.L. Keller (GOC), Lt Gen J.T. Crocker (GOC British I Corps), Brig P.A.S. Todd (CRCA), Brig K.G. Blackader (OC 8th Inf Bde), Brig D.G. Cunningham (OC 9th Inf Bde).*

Left: *An infantryman will always keep his rifle – and bayonet – clean. This soldier is from the North Shore (New Brunswick) Regiment on 8–9 June.*

Below Left: *3in mortar crew of Support Coy, Regina Rifles, during the battle of Bretteville-l'Orgueilleuse, 8–9 June; note three-round cardboard carrying tube.*

Below: *The 2in mortar fired a range of ammunition. Bombs had four-finned tails: HE, with an impact fuse in its nose, was painted olive with a red band; smoke was painted dark green; para illuminating flare was painted khaki; signal star (white, red, green, mixed red and green) was painted grey.*

THE ROYAL CANADIAN ARMY MEDICAL CORPS

Medical facilities and casualty evacuation had improved since World War I and had been considered carefully in the run up to D-Day. The proximity of UK hospitals and the plethora of craft meant there were ample opportunities to evacuate the wounded by sea. Once the lodgement on Normandy was large enough, hospitals were set up – in July Bayeux had become the location for a Nos 7, 8 and 10 general hospitals (capacity 2,400), there was also No 6 (capacity 200) at Douvres. Around 35,000 men and women (over 3,500 nursing sisters) had served with RCAMC by the end of the war. They treated 83,943 Canadians and upwards of 60,000 other Allied personnel. for wounds and sickness.

Above and Below: *Battlefield casualties were first tended in situ or at a regimental aid post – this sequence shows a chaplain and RAP of the Cameron Highlanders of Ottawa. The patients were then transported to the rear by jeep or other means (often stretcherbearers – note SB armband* **Below Left**). *There they were treated as far as possible at a casualty clearing post or, in the early stages, at the beach group medical station (***Opposite, Above Right***), before return to England by LST – in this case (***Opposite, Below Left***) on 8 June – where they were taken to suitable hospitals. Soon, however, advanced surgical centres were set up in Normandy combining field dressing stations, transfusion and surgical units.*

Centre Right: *After treatment, the casualty then went to convalesce at a casualty clearing station or general hospital. From 17 July there were nursing sisters of the RCAMC in France. These were the first to arrive after D-Day. Their presence was excellent for morale and they did a fine job close to the front line.*

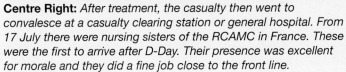

Below Right: *Around 1,400 padres of the Canadian Chaplain Service (note CCS on patch) served with Canadian forces in the war. As well as their spiritual ministry, they cared for casualties often in perilous positions. A number were killed in action – Capt W. Brown murdered as a PoW and Capt G.A. Harris KIA with1st Can Para Bn. Capt J.W. Foote won the VC at Dieppe, after carrying wounded to the landing craft and remaining on the beach following evacuation.*

Right and Inset: *The Canadians had been sitting outside Carpiquet airfield since early June and had planned an attack as part of Operation Epsom. Taking the airfield, particularly the southern side, was essential to protect British attacks through Hill 112. In the end, Operation Windsor started on 4 July with 8th Inf Bde, supported by the 10th Armd Regt (the Fort Garry Horse), the Royal Winnipeg Rifles, three squadrons of flails, Crocodiles and AVREs of 79th Armd Div, artillery as well as the naval guns of HMSs Rodney and Roberts and Typhoon fighter-bombers. The Germans however – mainly 1./SS-PzGr-Regt 26 of Hitlerjugend – had dug-in positions, good fields of fire over the locality, all covered by ranged artillery. They resisted defiantly. The initial attack stalled with heavy losses – 117 dead – and it was not until 8–9 July that Operation Trousers, part of Operation Charnwood, took the airfield.*

Below: *This memorial stands near Carpiquet airport.*

Opposite, Top: *A Sherman of the Fort Garry Horse near the wrecked hangars. The regiment lost 13 tanks in Operation Windsor but inflicted heavy casualties on 1.SS-Pz-Div Leibstandarte when the Germans counterattacked repeatedly on 5 July.*

Opposite, Below Left: *Men of the Queen's Own Rifles with their 6pdr ATk gun.*

THE ATTACK ON CARPIQUET
4 JULY 1944

NORTH SHORE REGIMENT

QUEEN'S OWN RIFLES OF CDA
MOVEMENT AT 11.00 AM

RÉGIMENT DE LA CHAUDIÈRE

Marcelet

ROYAL WINNIPEG RIFLES

8TH CANADIAN INFANTRY BRIGADE WITH
10TH CANADIAN ARMOURED REGT.
STARTLINE

OBJECTIVE N. SHORE R.

Carpiquet

OBJECTIVE R. DE CHAUD

HANGARS

OBJECTIVE Q.O.R. OF C.

AIRFIELD

CONTROL BUILDINGS

OBJECTIVE R. WPG RIF

HANGARS

1/2   MILE
Ground over 60 metres.....

MAIN BRITISH AND CANADIAN OPERATIONS IN NORMANDY 1944

Operation	Start	Mission
Neptune	06.06	Secure a lodgement on the continent of Europe
Perch	10.06	Advance towards Caen
Martlet	25.06	Securing right flank to help Op Epsom
Epsom	26.06	Advance towards Caen
Windsor	04.07	Attack on Carpiquet airfield
Charnwood	08.07	Advance towards Caen
Trousers	08.07	Taking Carpiquet airfield
Jupiter	10.07	Hill 112: stopping Panzers heading W
Greenline	25.07	Hill 113: stopping Panzers heading W
Pomegranate	16.07	Divert German attention from Operation Goodwood
Goodwood	18.07	Attack around east of Caen
Atlantic	18.07	Attack south of Caen
Spring	25.07	Attack on Verrières Ridge
COBRA	25.07	US BREAKOUT
Bluecoat	30.07	Protecting US V corps flank
Lüttich	*06.08*	*German counter-attack at Mortain*
Totalize	08.08	First major operation by First Canadian Army attacks towards Falaise
Tractable	14.08	Follow-up towards Falaise

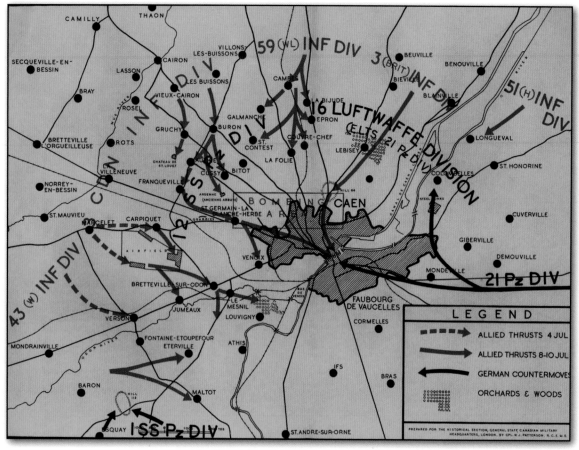

Left: *Operation Charnwood. On the western edge of the Allied lodgement US forces were fighting their way towards Saint-Lô. The Germans wanted to move armour west to stop them – what was left of Panzer Lehr began to move on 8 July. It was important that the British and Canadians continued to apply pressure in the east. They did so on 8 July through Operation Charnwood, attacking – after a massive bomber strike and heavy preparatory artillery fire – around Caen. The fighting was attritional: the Luftwaffe's 16. Feld-Division lost heavily as did the remnants of Hitler-jugend as they defended Gruchy, Buron and Authie. At Buron the Highland Light Infantry of Canada sustained 262 casualties on the 8th, with 62 dead. At Authie the North Nova Scotia Highlanders got their revenge for their losses on 7 June. Every advance had to prepare for immediate counter-attacks, but finally the Germans left the northern half of Caen on 9 July. As the population celebrated, so the Allies prepared for battles south of the Orne. The debate about the fall of Caen – too little, too late is one historian's verdict – misses the undoubted strategic affect. First, it maintained pressure in the east reducing the reinforcements that went west. Second, it vitalised French public opinion – liberation was on its way. Finally, it put the fear of God up the Germans! Von Rundstedt had already suggested they make peace. Within 10 days the 20 July bomb plot took place.*

Opposite, Below: *A camouflaged Sherman Firefly of 2nd Can Armd Bde near Buron.*

Top Left: *A damaged PzKpfw V from 4./SS-Pz-Regt 12 of* Hitlerjugend *near Authie.*

Left: *A KO'd PzKpfw IV at Gruchy – the village fell to the Stormont, Dundas and Glengarry Highlanders on 8 July.*

Top: *Supper at Authie on 9 July. The men are using a No 2 cooker, a single-burner in a folding case powered by pressurised petrol from a small tank.*

Above: *Taken after the battle for Buron, this is a 2in mortar crew of the Highland Light Infantry of Canada. Note in foreground the mortar's circular canvas cover.*

Right: *After Operation Charnwood was closed on 10 July, Lt Gen Miles Dempsey, GOC Second British Army, proposed the largest British tank attack in history – Operation Good- wood. If it were successful, then the Allies would be on their way to Paris; if not, then it would at least hold potential reinforcements in place in the east. It was launched with Montgomery under pressure to break out but knowing that his source of infantry replacements was running short. The Canadian element, Operation Atlantic, was undertaken by II Canadian Corps, newly operational. It was costly: 1,965 casualties with 441 dead. Of these, 1,349 were from the 2nd Can Inf Div, its first combat in Normandy.*

Below – L–R:

Sherman tanks of the Sherbrooke Fusilier Regt advancing through Caen

Infantrymen of the Highland Light Infantry of Canada rest in Caen before the start of the operation.

The North Nova Scotia Highlanders cross London Bridge, a Bailey bridge across the Odon River south of Caen, on 18 July.

A Humber Mk III light reconnaissance car in Caen.

Universal Carrier of the 4th Field Regt, RCA, 2nd Can Inf Bde in Vaucelles, around 20 July.

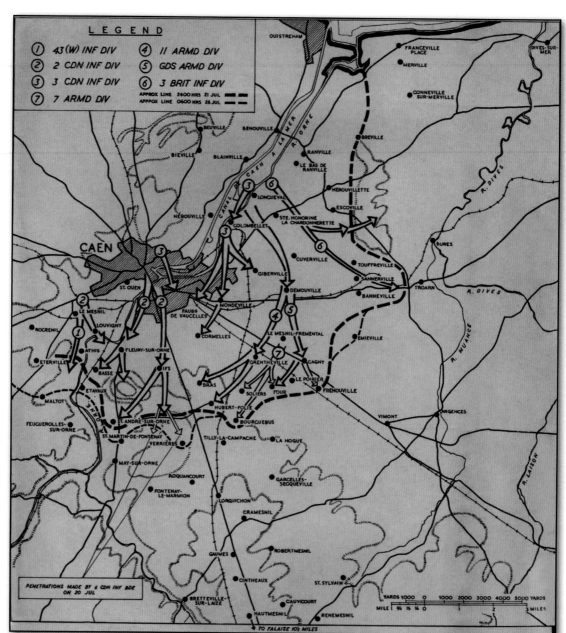

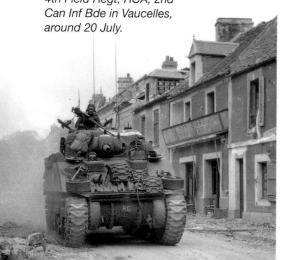

Three days of heavy fighting and losses of men and tanks saw the Operation Atlantic held just in front of the Verrières high ground. The fighting to take the ridge here – Operation Spring on 25–27 July – led to further serious Canadian casualties, in particular the Black Watch of Canada who suffered 315 casualties from its strength of 325 on 25 July. However, it kept the German Panzers in place as the US Operation Cobra started. By the time the Germans could send reinforcements west, it really was too little, too late. A major moment, however, had arrived for the Canadian forces in Normandy: First Canadian Army became operational on 23 July. Its first major battle was Operation Totalize on 8 August.

Left: *Men of the 8th Can Inf Bde (3rd Can Inf Div) wait to advance into the industrial area of Caen. In Operation Atlantic the division captured Caen's suburbs of Giberville and Vaucelles.*

Below: *RCA gunners clean a 5.5-inch gun south of Vaucelles, France, 23 July 1944.*

FIRST CANADIAN ARMY ORDER OF BATTLE FOR OPERATION TOTALIZE

ARMY TROOPS
F Sqn 25th Armd Delivery Regt (Elgin Regt)
1st Army Group, RCA
    11th Army Field Regt
    1st, 2nd and 5th Medium Regts
2nd Army Group, RCA
    19th Army Field Regt
    3rd, 4th and 7th Medium Regts
    2nd HAA Regt (Mobile)
HQ Defence Bn (Royal Montreal Regt)

I BRITISH CORPS (Lt Gen John Crocker)
Corps Troops
Inns of Court Regt, RAC (armoured cars)
    62nd Anti-Tank Regt, RA
    102nd LAA Regt, RA
    9th Survey Regt, RA
4th Army Group, RA
    150th (South Nottinghamshire Hussars Yeomanry) Field Regt, RA
    53rd (London), 65th, 68th and 79th (Scottish Horse Yeomanry)
      Medium Regts, RA
    51st (Lowland) Heavy Regt, RA

51st (Highland) Infantry Division
6th Airborne Division (returned to UK 3 September 1944)
49th (West Riding) Infantry Division
7th Armoured Division

Supporting units from the RE, RCS, RAOC, RASC, RAMC

II CANADIAN CORPS (Lt Gen Guy Simonds)
Corps Troops
II Canadian Corps Defence Coy (Prince Edward Island Light Horse)
18th Armd Car Regt (12th Manitoba Dragoons)
2nd Corps Defence Coy (Prince Edward Island Light Horse)
6th Anti-Tank Regt, RCA
2nd Survey Regt, RCA
6th LAA Regt, RCA

2nd Infantry Division (Maj Gen Charles Foulkes)
8th Recce Regt (14th Canadian Hussars)
4th Infantry Brigade
    Royal Regt of Canada
    Royal Hamilton Light Infantry
    Essex Scottish Regt
5th Infantry Brigade
    Black Watch (Royal Highland Regt) of Canada
    Régiment de Maisonneuve
    Calgary Highlanders
6th Infantry Brigade
    Fusiliers Mont-Royal
    Queen's Own Cameron Highlanders of Canada
    South Saskatchewan Regt
Toronto Scottish Regt (MG)
4th, 5th and 6th Field Regts, RCA
2nd Anti-Tank Regt, RCA
3rd LAA Regt, RCA

3rd Infantry Division (Maj Gen Rod Keller)
7th Recce Regt (17th Duke of York's Royal Canadian Hussars)
7th Infantry Brigade
    Royal Winnipeg Rifles
    Regina Rifle Regt
    1st Bn, Canadian Scottish Regt
8th Infantry Brigade
    Queen's Own Rifles of Canada
    Régiment de la Chaudière
    North Shore (New Brunswick) Regt
9th Infantry Brigade
    Highland Light Infantry of Canada
    Stormont, Dundas and Glengarry Highlanders
    North Nova Scotia Highlanders
Cameron Highlanders of Ottawa (MG)
12th, 13th and 14th Field Regts, RCA
3rd Anti-Tank Regt, RCA
4th LAA Regt, RCA

4th Armoured Division (Maj Gen Harry Foster)
9th Armd Recce Regt (South Alberta Regt)
4th Armd Brigade
    21st Armd Regt (Governor General's Foot Guards)
    22nd Armd Regt (Canadian Grenadier Guards)
    28th Armd Regt (British Columbia Regt)
    Lake Superior Regt (Motor)
10th Infantry Brigade
    10th Independent MG Coy (New Brunswick Rangers)
    Lincoln and Welland Regt
    Algonquin Regt
    Argyll and Sutherland Highlanders of Canada (Princess Louise's)
15th and 23rd (SP) Field Regts, RCA
5th Anti-Tank Regt, RCA
8th LAA Regt, RCA
D Sqn, 25th Armd Delivery Regt (Elgin Regt)

2nd Canadian Armd Brigade (Brig Robert Wyman)
    6th Armd Regt (1st Hussars)
    10th Armd Regt (Fort Garry Horse)
    27th Armd Regt (Sherbrooke Fusilier Regt)
    C Sqn, 25th Armd Delivery Regt (Elgin Regt)

1st Polish Armoured Division (Maj Gen Stanisław Maczek)
10th Armoured Cavalry Brigade (Col T. Majewski)
1st and 2nd Armoured Regts
24th Polish Uhlan Regt (Armd)
10th Dragoons Regt

3rd Infantry Brigade (Col M. Wieronski)
1st Podhale Rifles, 8th and 9th Rifle Bns
1st Polish Independent HMG Sqn

Divisional Artillery
1st and 2nd Motorized Artillery Regt
1st AA Regt

10th Mounted Rifle Regt (armoured recce with Cromwell tanks)

Supporting units from the RCE, RCCS, RCAOC, RCASC, RCAMC

First Canadian Army formed in early 1942 and trained hard under original commander Andrew McNaughton. However, because of lack of opportunities for action, I Canadian Corps was hived off to fight in the Mediterranean. This meant that the army in Normandy was always composed of international units – particularly 1st Polish Armd Div and I British Corps, but also Belgians, Dutch, Czechs and even Americans. By the end of the war it comprised the largest army ever to be handled by a Canadian general. Postwar, it hasn't always received the plaudits it perhaps should have done for its hard fighting in poor conditions – such as the Channel ports, the Breskens Pocket, the Scheldt and on the Maas in the horrible winter of 1944–45.

Right: Harry Crerar was not always the easiest of commanding officers and both John Crocker and Guy Simonds had arguments with him.

Below Right: Guy Simonds was aged only 41 when he became GOC II Canadian Corps. He was an unlikeable but brilliant soldier who pushed new ideas such as the APC 'battle taxis'.

Below: Crocker (right, with I Corps insignia on his arm) and Keller, GOC 3rd Canadian Infantry Division. Crocker commanded the landings on Juno and Sword Beaches and over the Orne.

THE FALAISE GAP

First Canadian Army took the field just as Hitler made two major strategic decisions. First, he had finally decided that there was to be no attack from England over the Pas de Calais and had moved troops from Fifteenth Armee to help defend against the Allied thrust. What this meant was that two fully equipped German front-line infantry divisions arrived to bolster the defence – 89. Inf-Div (on 4 August) and 85. Inf-Div (on the 10th).

Hitler's second decision had also become apparent when on 6 August the new Oberbefehlshaber West (von Rundstedt had been replaced as German Commander-in-Chief West by GFM Günther von Kluge in early July) launched Operation Lüttich, an armoured attack planned to cut the western corridor the Americans had blown open with Operation Cobra. He did so with what was left of four armoured divisions, and the Americans were able to parry the attack efficiently, although it got to within two miles of Avranches and required heroic defence by 30th (US) Infantry Division who suffered heavy casualties. The Germans stuck their necks out and had created their own trap.

After all the fighting around Caen and Saint-Lô, in early August the Allies were close to success. Patton's Third Army had been unleashed into the weakly protected hinterland and was

speeding around the southern end of the German salient created by Lüttich. The British Operation Bluecoat had broken through towards Vire and was pressurising the northern side. South of Caen the Germans were still defending in depth with the fresh 85. and 89. Inf-Divs swelling the defenders' ranks, but Lt Gen Guy Simonds, GOC II Canadian Corps, had a cunning plan. He had the 105mm main armament taken out of M7 Priest SP guns and converted them into 'defrocked Priests'. They lined up in six columns and Operation Totalize saw them advance behind a rolling artillery barrage before dismounting close to their objectives. Verrières Ridge was taken and the attack advanced 10 miles towards Falaise.

From north and south two great pincers were closing around the neck of the salient with most of the German forces in Normandy inside. The only question was how many would be able to get out before the pincers – spearheaded in the north by two units that had only just entered the battle, 1st Polish and 4th Canadian Armd Divs – could close. The Germans fought ferociously, but left a lot of men and most of their heavy weapons behind. Crucially, however, sufficient HQ and senior admin cadres survived to head up new units in the Low Countries.

Opposite, Above Left:
*A Sherbrooke Fusilier
Sherman – possibly 'Bomb'
(see p159), in Falaise, August
1944 with troops of the
Fusiliers Mont-Royal.*

Opposite, Above Right:
*Simonds converted some 60
Priests into APCs for Operation
Totalize – these are being used
by 1st Bn, Black Watch
of Canada.*

**Opposite, Below Right and
Left:** *Soldiers of Les Fusiliers
Mont-Royal inspect KO'd
PzKpfw V Ausf Gs – both from
Hitlerjugend. One is from KG
Wünsche on 8 August (**Left**)
– in the Grimbosq bridgehead
– and the other (**Right**) is in St
André-sur-Orne on 9 August.*

Right: *Operation Totalize
opened on 8 August and
marked the beginning of the
First Canadian Army thrust that
would trap the Germans in the
Falaise Pocket.*

Below: *Polish Cromwells
advance towards Falaise.
Unfortunately, Totalize lost
traction as 1st Polish and 4th
Can Armd Divs prepared to
attack, when USAAF B-17s
bombed short inflicting
casualties to both divisions.
Indeed, the North Shore Regt
near Caen lost nearly 100 men
and the GOC 3rd Inf Div, Rod
Keller, was badly wounded.
Then the Germans counter-
attacked with help from the
Tigers of sSS-Pz-Abt 101. In
this attack, Joe Ekins of the 1st
Northants Yeomanry knocked
out four tanks – including three
Tigers, one of which belonged
to SS-pinup Michael Wittmann.*

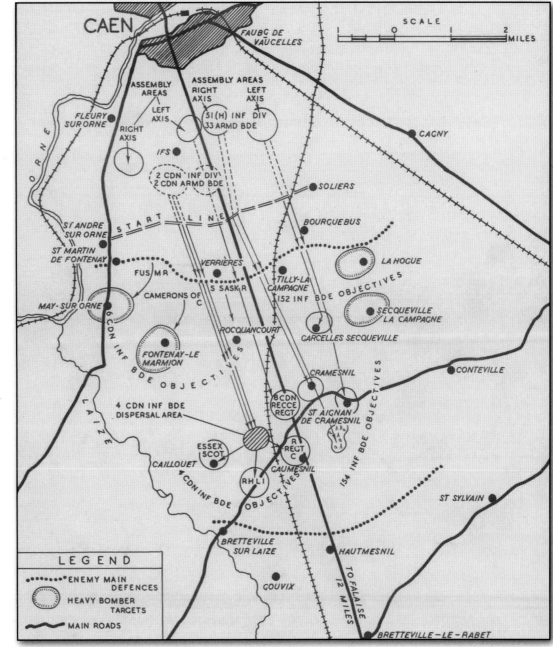

1ST POLISH ARMOURED DIVISION

1st Polish Armd Div arrived in France at the end of July (as the stele on Juno Beach testifies **Below**) and became part of First Canadian Army. Its first taste of combat was in Operation Totalize and the Poles acquitted themselves with their usual courage and elan. Their commanding officer was Maj Gen Stanisław Maczek who was greatly loved by his men. They called him 'Baca' – a traditional Polish name for a shepherd. After Poland fell, Maczek, then a colonel, escaped with the remnants of his brigade and, after a short time in France, ended up in Britain where Polish 1st Armd Div was formed. Introduced into action during Operation Totalize, the Poles made a tentative start and were criticised for their slow speed south – although they were green troops beside the British and Canadian men who had been fighting since early June, and their heroism on Hill 262 was apparent to all. The memorials that follow the division through France, Belgium and the Netherlands attest to the friends that the Poles made on their 10-month campaign. In particular, the people of Breda remember Maczek who was buried there after the war.

Sur les plages d'Arromanches et Graye/Courseulles, fin juillet 1944, 16000 soldats et 400 chars de la 1ère Division Blindée Polonaise ont débarqué avec à leur tête le Général Stanisław MACZEK.

"Pour notre et votre liberté"

Na plażach Arromanches i Graye/Courseulles, pod koniec lipca 1944, wylądowało 16000 żołnierzy i 400 czołgów, Polskiej 1. Dywizji Pancernej na czele z generałem Stanisławem MACZKIEM

"Za wolność naszą i waszą"

Left: *Happy to be here! Men of the division on the day before Operation Totalize began, 7 July.*

Below Left: *At the First Canadian Army HQ, Amblie, 7 August, Maj Gen Stanisław Maczek briefs army press correspondents about the forthcoming operation.*

Right: *Tanks of the Polish division lined up ready to strike south in the second phase of Operation Totalize. Note the PL marking on the rear of the Sherman Vc Firefly. The 51 would have been on a red background and identifies 1st Polish Armd Regt – the senior regiment of the 10th Armd Cavalry Bde. (52 would signify the 2nd Polish Armd Regt and 53 the 24th Pol Lancer Regt.)*

Below: *1st Polish Armd Div's insignia harks back to the famous 'Winged Hussars' of the 16th and 17th centuries.*

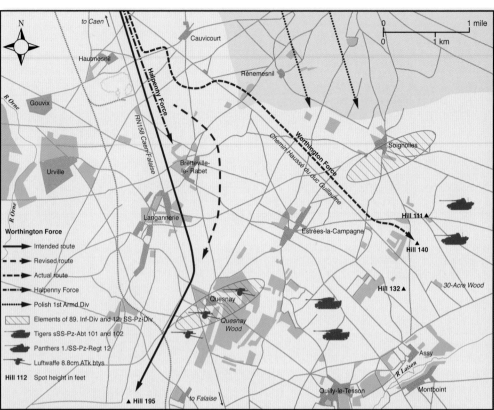

Some of the bombs that were supposed to help start the second part of Operation Totalize dropped on the troops they were planned to help (**Opposite, Above Right**). The operation was halted almost in its tracks by this and laagered up for the night. Guy Simonds attempted to restart the operation by pushing a night attack on Hill 195 (see map **Above Right**). It all went horribly wrong, and the battlegroup, Worthington Force, made up of tanks of the British Columbia Regt and infantry of the Algonquin Regt, ran into and was destroyed by nearby German armour. This was the first time these troops – and the supporting Poles – had seen action and this may have contributed to the difficulties, because Worthington Force missed its path in the night, went astray and was unable to communicate its position to get artillery support, although it was fortunate enough to get some assistance from Typhoon fighter-bombers which had attacked the battlegroup first. Had the Canadians had the same tactical air setup that the US/USAAF had worked out, the end might have been different. As it was, the force sustained 240 casualties and lost nearly 40 tanks. Today there's a memorial to the brave men of Worthington Force near where they made their last stand (**Above Left**). Their objective, Hill 195, was taken the next night (10 August) by 1st Bn, Argyll and Sutherland Highlanders of Canada. The annihilation of Worthington Force lost Simonds a real

chance of a breakthrough, as Meyer's Hitlerjugend was stretched very thin. It has been argued that a more enterprising commander could have smashed through by supporting Worthington Force but a combination of bad luck, poor communications, lack of battle experience and a dogged defence saw the opportunity missed.

Opposite, Above Left: Operation Tractable started on 14 August and pushed First Canadian Army across the River Laison. Three days later Falaise fell. But the so-called Falaise Gap had moved southeast, now lying between Trun and Argentan, and the fighting was intensifying as the Germans began a pell-mell retreat and the Americans advanced from the south to Chambois.

Opposite, Centre Left: The memorial at Clair Tison (or Tizon) to the Calgary Highlanders remembers taking the bridge over the Laize on 13 August. (It's to the W of Fontaine-Le-Pin off the map **Opposite, Above Left.** NB R Laize heads north and joins the R Orne; R Laison heads northeast and joins the R Dives.)

Opposite, Below Left and Right: Heavy fighting took place on 14 August along the Laison River, a major obstacle to the Canadians, until bridges could be laid as here at Rouvres.

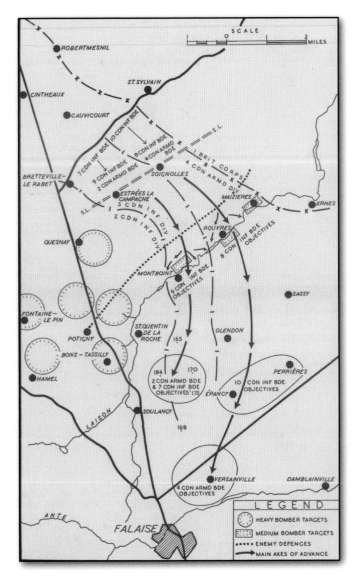

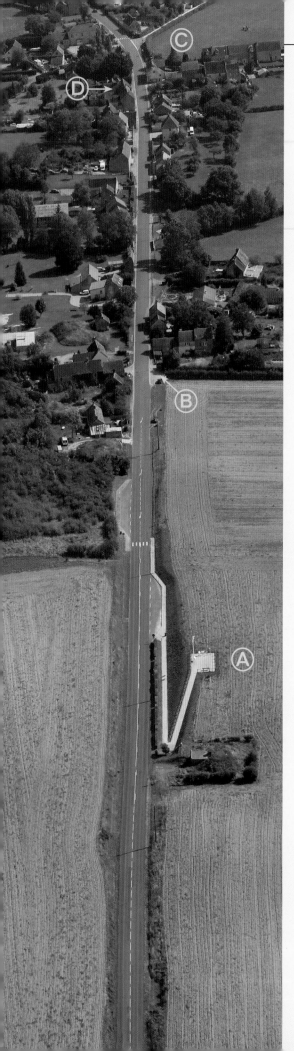

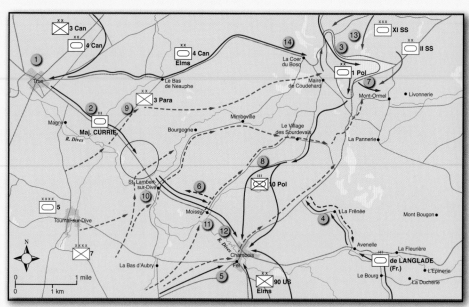

THE GAP CLOSES

August 18

1 The Canadians (3rd Inf and 4th Armd Divs) capture Trun. The gap is around five miles wide.

2 Maj David Currie's 4th Can Armd Div battlegroup (made up at various times of a squadron of the South Alberta Regt, units of B Coy, the Argyll and Sutherland Highlanders of Canada, the Lincoln and Welland Regt and the 5th Anti-Tank Regt) takes Hill 117 and heads toward St-Lambert-sur-Dive. The aerial view (**Left**) looks SE down the main street of St-Lambert. At **A** the viewing platform. At **B** a memorial to Currie whose battlegroup fought to keep the pocket closed, accounting for 3,000 Germans killed, wounded or captured. At **C** the roads heading towards the bridges over the Dives.

3 1st Polish Armd Div takes the heights overlooking the German escape route.

4 Groupe de Langlade of French 2e DB advances on La Frênée to block the Germans on Route 16, but turns back with orders to be ready to rush to liberate Paris, which happens on 24 August.

5 Elements of 90th (US) Inf Div move out of Argentan and recapture Le Bourg-St Léonard, providing artillery spotting locations from the ridge. They attack Chambois and Fel.

August 19

6 4th Can Armd Div tries to link with US forces in Chambois.

7 1st Polish Armd Div attacks towards the Americans around Chambois.

8 10th Polish Mounted Rifles reach Chambois at 19:00 linking with US troops but in insufficient force to keep the pocket – holding remnants of 15 German divisions – closed.

9 Gen Meindl's 3. Fallschirmjäger-Division (II.FJ-Korps) holds the left flank.

August 20

10 Kurt Meyer and 12. SS-Pz-Div HQ breaks out around 01:00.

11 Elements of XLVII. Pz-Korps and I. SS-Pz-Korps break out under cover of darkness.

12 Canadian forces join up with American and Polish forces, temporarily sealing the gap.

13 German counter-attacks to reopen the pocket. What remains of 2. and 9. SS-Pz-Divisionen attack the Poles from outside the pocket. The battles on Hill 262 from the night of 19/20 August, are intense. Around midday elements of 10. SS, 12. SS, and 116. Pz-Divisionen manage to escape.

August 21

14 The night of 20/21 is the hardest for the beleaguered Poles, but elements of the 4th Can Armd arrive at dawn to relieve the pressure on Hill 262. Fighting stops in Chambois. 2,000 Germans surrender in Tournai-sur-Dive. The battle is effectively over.

Top: *The monument at the Mémorial de Montormel on the heights of Hill 262 honours 1st Polish Armd Div, Can 4th Armd Div and Grenadier Guards, French 2e DB and the 359th Inf Regt of US 90th Inf Div. The two armoured vehicles are a 2e DB M8 Greyhound (right) and an M4A1(76)W Sherman named* Maczuga *(left). The name means mace in English and this is what the Poles called the position on Mont Ormel ridge.*

Above: *Jagdpanther and Sherman knocked out in the fighting on the Mace. Lt-Col Aleksander Stefanowicz's 1st Armd Regt held Hill 262 between 19 and 21 August. They were relieved by the arrival of the Canadian Grenadier Guards at 14:00 on the 21st.*

Right: *David Currie (at left, holding revolver) was awarded the VC for his valour during the fighting in the village 18–19 August. Currie's battle group fought for three days to keep the Falaise pocket closed. View looking northwest towards Trun, the house at right indicated at* **D** *on the aerial photo.*

Right: *The channel of the German retreat was squeezed by the attacking Allies until only a small corridor existed between St-Lambert-sur-Dive and Chambois. This aerial photograph mirrors the map opposite and shows one of the crossing points of the R Dives, today a rural ford* **(Opposite, Below Right)**. *The main road at the top of the photo and map is the D13 and the Germans were heading NE – straight towards the cork in the bottle: the Poles' position atop Hill 262 (at* **A** *on the map below).*
Supreme Allied Commander Gen Dwight D. Eisenhower walked the area and talked about 'scenes that could be described only by Dante.' The Canadians had lost 389 officers and 5,795 ORs dead, wounded or missing since the start of Operation Totalize on 7 August. Prisoners totalled over 18,000. It was a massive victory.

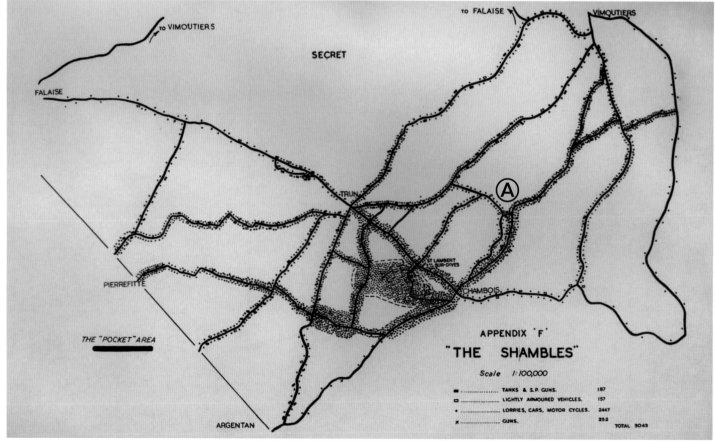

APPENDIX 'F'

"THE SHAMBLES"

Scale 1:100,000

■	TANKS & S.P. GUNS.	187
▭	LIGHTLY ARMOURED VEHICLES.	157
•	LORRIES, CARS, MOTOR CYCLES.	2447
X	GUNS.	252
		TOTAL 3043

THE "POCKET" AREA

TO VIMOUTIERS

TO FALAISE   VIMOUTIERS

SECRET

FALAISE

TRUN

ST LAMBERT SUR-DIVES

CHAMBOIS

PIERREFITTE

ARGENTAN

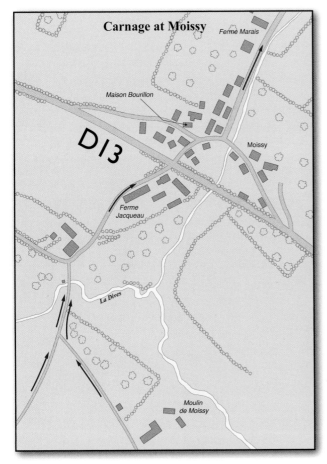

Carnage at Moissy

Ferme Marais

Maison Bourillon

D13

Moissy

Ferme Jacqueau

La Dives

Moulin de Moissy

B-548

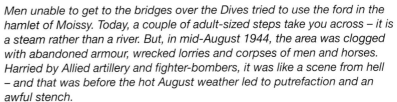

Men unable to get to the bridges over the Dives tried to use the ford in the hamlet of Moissy. Today, a couple of adult-sized steps take you across – it is a steam rather than a river. But, in mid-August 1944, the area was clogged with abandoned armour, wrecked lorries and corpses of men and horses. Harried by Allied artillery and fighter-bombers, it was like a scene from hell – and that was before the hot August weather led to putrefaction and an awful stench.

RCAF SQUADRONS IN 2TAF

No 83 Group, RAF had a big RCAF contingent and by August 1944 was operating out of French landing strips. While in the aftermath of Operation Lüttich and the Falaise Gap battles there were claims that Allied airpower had been the crucial factor, today we know that tank-busting was less successful than claimed and most losses were down to gunfire, abandonment as a result of automotive unreliability or lack of fuel. However, against men and soft-skinned vehicles the fighter-bombers were deadly. In the first two weeks of August No 406 Sqn claimed 117 vehicles destroyed; No 442 on the 13th claimed 60 vehicles and 10 tanks; and on the 14th 75 vehicles and 11 tanks and AFVs. The aircraft were more likely to run out of ammo than targets. On the 18th 2TAF claimed over 3,000 vehicles destroyed. However, the fight was not entirely one-sided. German Flak over the battlefield was intense and the memorial at Noyers Bocage (**Opposite**) is dedicated to the Typhoon pilots – over 150 of them – who died over Normandy.

Right: *2TAF was established on 1 June 1943 and its No 143 Wing on 10 January 1944. Made up of Nos 438, 439 and 440 Sqn, RCAF its role was fighter-ground attack to support the Canadian and British troops of 21st Army Group. From 22/23 June to 30 August 1944 the wing was located at B.5 (Fresne Camille) (for two days only) and then Lantheuil (B.9), just south of Creully, before moving forward to keep up with the ground forces Here No 440 Sqn men pose with a 'Tiffie' at Lantheuil. (The bomber versions were nicknamed 'Bombphoons'.)*

Below: *Typhoon Mk IB 'P' of No 438 Sqn at Lantheuil.*

Left: *No 440 Sqn, RCAF had a varied career starting the war as No 111 (Coast Artillery Co-Operation) Sqn at Patricia Bay on Vancouver Island. Redesignated No 111 (Fighter) Sqn on 1 July 1940, it was disbanded in February 1941 and then reformed on 3 November 1941 flying the Curtis Kittyhawk. It took part in air defence operations in the Aleutian Islands Campaign claiming one kill – the only Japanese fighter by the RCAF home air force during the war. The squadron moved to RAF Ayr in Scotland where it was redesignated No 440 (Fighter Bomber) Sqn on 8 February 1944, beginning operations on 30 March with Typhoons out of RAF Hurn. Here two of its aircraft show off their missile armament.*

Right: *This splendid memorial is on the site of the B.2 Bazenville ALG used 16 June– 15 August by Nos 403, 416 and 421 Sqns, RCAF. It's in the shape of a Spitfire wing.*

Bottom: *This memorial to Typhoon pilots who fought during the battle of Normandy is at Noyers Bocage.*

3 Clearing the Coast

Ⓐ →

In the heady days after the Falaise Pocket closed, the Allies raced across France and Belgium at a rate unimaginable during the hard-fought battles around Caen or in the bocage. The battle of Normandy had been a pressure cooker, and once the seal was released, the German defences collapsed. For the Allies, the problems were those of managing success: their strategy and logistics. For the Germans, it appeared, there was nothing left but headlong flight: rearguard actions and an attempt to set up some sort of defence line – the Seine was the first and most obvious; after that, the canals and rivers of the Low Countries and then the German border itself, the Westwall.

It must have been very easy to think that the Wehrmacht was beaten when elements of Second British Army entered Antwerp on 4 September, First (US) Army reached Maastricht by the 14th and Aachen, in Germany itself, on the 12th. Certainly it was with this uppermost in their minds that Eisenhower – as of 1 September he had taken back control of all the ground forces – and his generals discussed strategy. The decision to try to bounce the Rhine via Arnhem was not the only option: Bradley and Patton were vociferous in their pleas to be allowed the primary thrust, and with US manpower now beginning to dominate the theatre it was difficult to say no. Eisenhower, however, gave Montgomery his opportunity. The ambitious thrust to flank the Westwall from the north failed. The advances slowed until Hitler stuck his neck out again in the Ardennes in December and allowed the Allies a second chance to wring it.

The critical period for the Allies' management of their victory in Normandy was the early weeks in September. It was in this period that they outran the supply lines that had been predicated on success – but not that much success. In the planning for Overlord, a port was to be constructed near Quiberon in Brittany – one of the reasons for Third Army's attacks in that direction – but the defeat of the German Army in France meant that Brittany was now too far from the action. Success in southern France saw Marseilles quickly operational, allowing Sixth (US) Army Group to benefit, but it was obvious that a Channel port was needed. Would it have been better to clear the Scheldt and open up Antwerp rather than attempt to win the war in 1944 via Arnhem? Possibly, but it is understandable that the Allies wanted to keep chasing what they saw as a beaten enemy – and

Opposite: *Three of the Todt Battery's four casemates are visible in the aerial photograph. The second is in the trees as indicated (A). Housing Krupp SK C/34 38cm (15-inch) guns capable of firing some 35 miles, the casemates were operational from mid-1942.*

Below: *The German collapse saw the Allies canter to the Seine, but it would be wrong to assume that there was no defense. It took eight days of fighting to reach the river, during which time the Germans were able to get many of their troops – and some of their heavy equipment – across. Two weeks later, First Canadian Army was on the Ghent Canal, at which point the advance began to stall as fatigue, logistical problems and a tougher German defence slowed the Allies.*

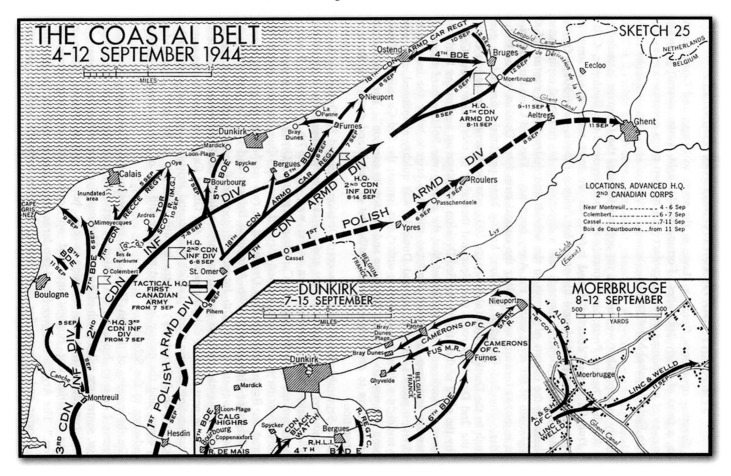

it must also be acknowledged that clearing the Scheldt would not have been as straightforward in September as is sometimes imagined. German Fifteenth Armee had had two infantry divisions mauled during Operations Totalize and Tractable but it still had a significant number of men in the area. With hindsight, in early September the biggest problem for the Allies was not logistics but the fact that during the period 7–23 September the Germans were able to save that army. Pallud (2007) gives the figures: 86,100 men, 616 guns, 6,200 vehicles, 6,200 horses and 6,500 bicycles escaped over the Scheldt. Elements of these units would survive to fight the Allies from Veghel to Wesel.

How did they get away? Because the Germans had managed to hold the land bridge from Walcheren to the mainland open and the Allies, surprisingly, weren't able to push forward from Antwerp to close it off. There were a number of reasons for this: first, they were looking towards Arnhem rather than Antwerp; second, First Canadian Army was clearing the Channel coast and held up on the Leopold Canal; third, the organisational performance of key German staff in the Breskens area who were able to manage the shipping assets so effectively; and finally, the crucial defence along the Albert Canal set up by Generalleutnant Kurt Chill around 4 September – as is brilliantly outlined by Jack Didden in his work on Kampfgruppe Chill and the German recovery.

Why wasn't First Canadian Army pushing harder? The feeling that the Canadians were dilatory isn't really born out by the facts. The Germans had set up defence lines along canals. Attacking these and defended cities isn't easy. The Americans had found the fortress ports they attacked difficult propositions. The Canadians, tasked with freeing the smaller Channel ports, had smaller opposition to contend with but it was still no pushover:

Location	Date of siege	Allied Casualties	Captured
Le Havre	10–12.09	under 500	11,000
Boulogne	17–22.09	600	10,000
Cap Gris Nez/Calais	22.09–1.10	260	9,128

Clearing the Channel ports took time and when Market Garden ended and all eyes turned to the Scheldt, the Germans had had time to ferry their Fifteenth Armee to safety and consolidate the already significant defences of the two fortresses – Schelde Süd and Walcheren. The consequent battles are covered in Chapter 4.

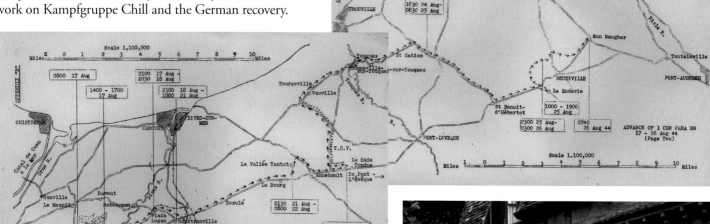

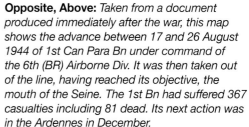

Opposite, Above: *Taken from a document produced immediately after the war, this map shows the advance between 17 and 26 August 1944 of 1st Can Para Bn under command of the 6th (BR) Airborne Div. It was then taken out of the line, having reached its objective, the mouth of the Seine. The 1st Bn had suffered 367 casualties including 81 dead. Its next action was in the Ardennes in December.*

Opposite, Below Left: *Unlike 1st Para Bn, First Canadian Army was further south and advanced towards the Seine from the Chambois area. It freed many towns such as this as it progressed – Bernay in Eure was liberated by 4th Can Armd Div on 24 August.*

Opposite, Below Right: *Canadians of the Royal Hamilton Light Infantry meet the US Army's 2nd Armored Division at Elbeuf, 27 August 1944. Leaving the Chambois area on the 23rd, some RHLI elements crossed the Seine at Criquebeuf on the 26/27th but opposition intensified and most units crossed at Elbeuf.*

Above Left: *Lt Gen Guy Simonds watches tanks of the Canadian Grenadier Guards crossing the Seine at Elbeuf on 28 August 1944.*

Left and Below Left: *Rouen's Boieldieu Bridge was of no help to the fleeing Germans nor the advancing Allies. The city was liberated by First Canadian Army on 30 August. Note Nebelwerfer at left.*

Below: *Canadian armoured cars – in front a Humber LRC, behind a Daimler – near the Seine.*

Below: *Le Havre was completely flattened by bombing and the fighting – Operation Astonia by I British Corps of First Canadian Army – lasted 10–12 September. This photo was taken later that year in the winter. So many civilians died that it became policy to let them leave other besieged locations before the fighting began.*

Bottom Left: *On 3 September – two days after it had liberated the town of Dieppe – 2nd Can Inf Div held a Victory Parade and memorial service to those who died in the 1942 raid. After this they moved to Dunkirk.*

Bottom Right: *Hitler declared a number of locations fortresses – Festungen – that had to fight to the last round. He also expected ports to ensure their facilities were destroyed to deny them to the Allies. Cherbourg's 20,000 defenders held out against American attacks from 22 to 29 June and its harbour was wrecked; Saint-Malo from 5 to 17 August. Brest was larger and better defended by over 45,000 men. It held out 7 August–19 September and caused the Americans 9,831 casualties. After that, the western Atlantic locations, the Channel Islands and Dunkirk were simply masked and 200,000 Germans sat idly by until the overall surrender.*

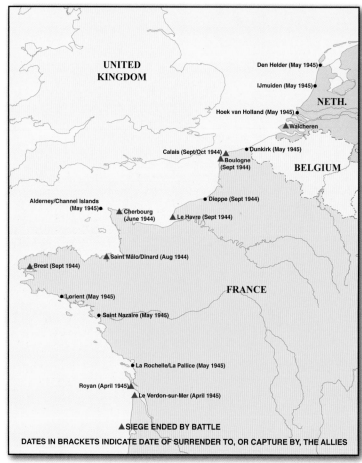

FLYING BOMB SITES

The flying bomb campaign of 1944 was not just terrifying, but did significant damage. The threat – particularly to civilian morale – made clearing the launch sites an important task. 9,521 of the shorter-range V1s were fired at the UK June–October 1944. Thereafter, they were directed at Antwerp and other targets in Belgium: 2,448 were launched up till 29 March 1945. The more deadly V2 was launched first against Paris on 8 September 1944. By war's end, nearly 3,200 others had followed, killing c. 9,000 civilians and military personnel mainly in London, Antwerp and Liege.

Centre Left: *Map showing the launching sites as identified in January 1944.*

Bottom Left: *This V1 ski-ramp launch site was at Almelo in the Netherlands. The last of the weapons was launched from here on 30 March 1945*

Below: *A crater caused by a V1 or V2 explosion, Fort de Merxim, Belgium, 15 October 1944.*

The attack on Boulogne started on 17 September. Having taken Le Tréport, the 3rd Can Inf Div moved up the coast to Boulogne which had the sizeable coastal artillery assets of MMA 240. These included the three massive 30.5cm guns of Friedrich August Battery located at Wimille-Le Trésorerie and Boulogne's batteries at Fort de la Creche Ouest, Fort Le Portel (Cap d'Alprech and Mont de Couppe batteries) as well as the 8.8cm guns on the harbour breakwater. The city was liberated by Operation Wellhit. First, the high ground to the southeast – Mont Lambert, that dominates the city – needed to be taken. Helped by the AVREs and Crocodiles of 79th Armd Div, the infantry carried in defrocked Priests, most of Mont Lambert (off photo at **A**) was in Canadian hands by the end of the first day. The 8th and 9th Inf Bdes continued the attack and after six days' hard fighting the garrison surrendered. The final outliers, Forts Le Portel and Outreau, threw in the towel after the commander Generalleutnant Ferdinand Heim was captured on the 22nd. The taking prisoner of over 200 officers showed that military realism meant more than the pledge they had signed to fight 'to the end of my life and that of the last man under me.'

Bottom, L–R:
Bombs fall on Mont Lambert.

German soldiers march off to prison camp. In the background is the dome of Boulogne Basilica, some 101m tall (**B**).

Personnel of C Coy, Stormont, Dundas and Glengarry Highlanders of Canada advancing on the fort at Le Portel, on 22 September.

Below: *That's how close to England Cap Gris Nez is. Those are the White Cliffs of Dover about 20 miles away. When France fell in 1940, the Germans built coastal gun batteries to use against shipping and to bombard Britain. They could have supported an invasion, instead they terrorised the good people of Kent, killing more than 200 civilians and damaging over 10,000 properties*

Above Right: *Battery Lindemann at Sangatte was the flagship of the coastal batteries. Today its bunkers are covered by the spoil from the nearby Channel Tunnel.*

Below Right: *The Atlantic Wall Museum is housed in one of the four huge Battery Todt casemates, that used to hold 38cm guns.*

As well as the coastal batteries, Eisenbahn-Batterien – *railway guns* – were sited along the Channel coast. This example (**Above**) outside the Atlantic Wall Museum is a 28cm K5 that could fire a 562lb (255kg) shell over 38 miles (62,000m).

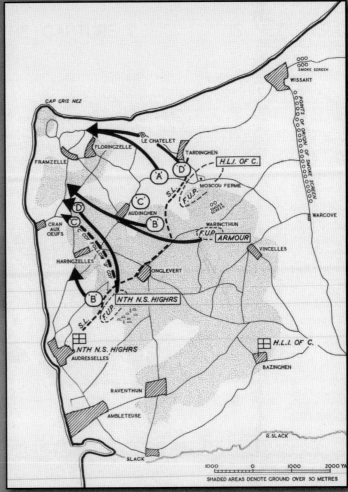

Above: *Between 22 September and 1 October, 3rd Can Inf Div took Calais and Cap Gris Nez in Operation Undergo, the 7th and 8th Inf Bdes attacking Calais and the 9th Cap Gris Nez. They captured nearly 10,000 troops and silenced the guns of MAA 242 and 244. Note the use of a smokescreen south of Wissant (top right in map) to hide what was going on from the garrison at Calais.*

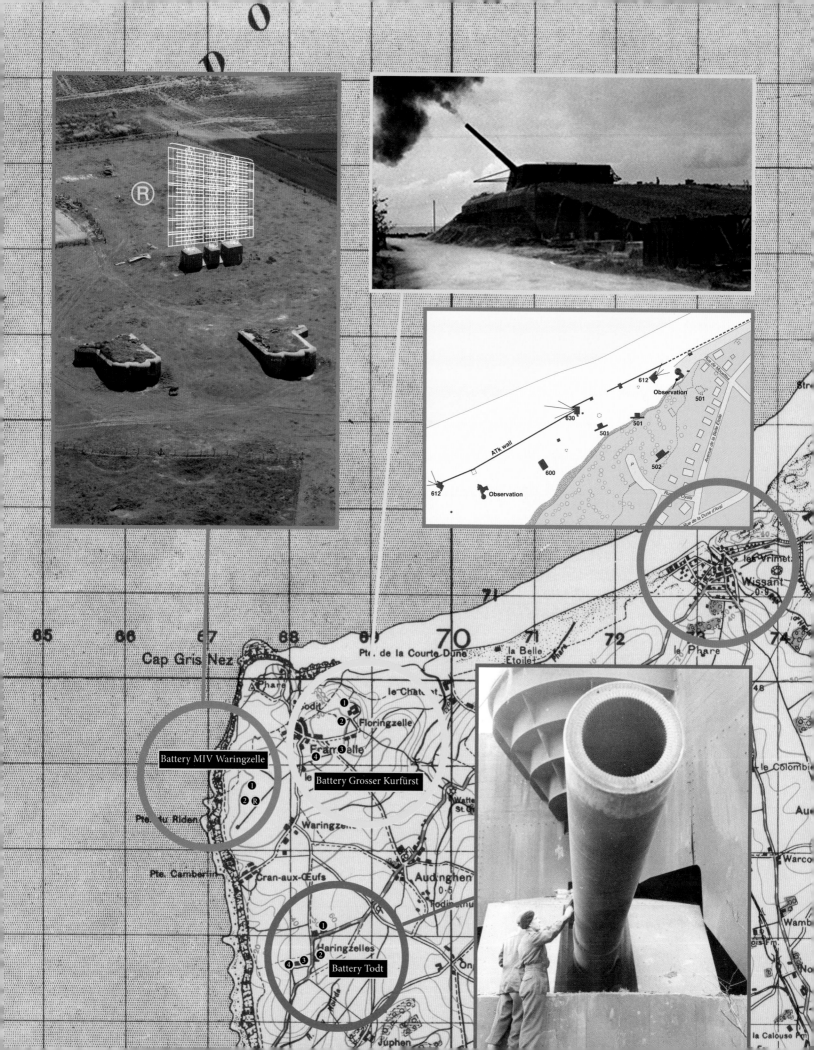

®

612
Observation
530
501
501
ATk wall
600
502
612
Observation

les Vrimet
Wissant

65   66   67   68   69   70   71   72   74

Cap Gris Nez   Pte. de la Courte Dune   la Belle Etoile   le Phare

le Chatel

Floringzelle

Framzelle

Battery MIV Waringzelle

Battery Grosser Kurfürst

Pte. du Riden

Waringzelle

Pte. Camberlin

Cran-aux-Œufs   Audinghen

Haringzelles

Battery Todt

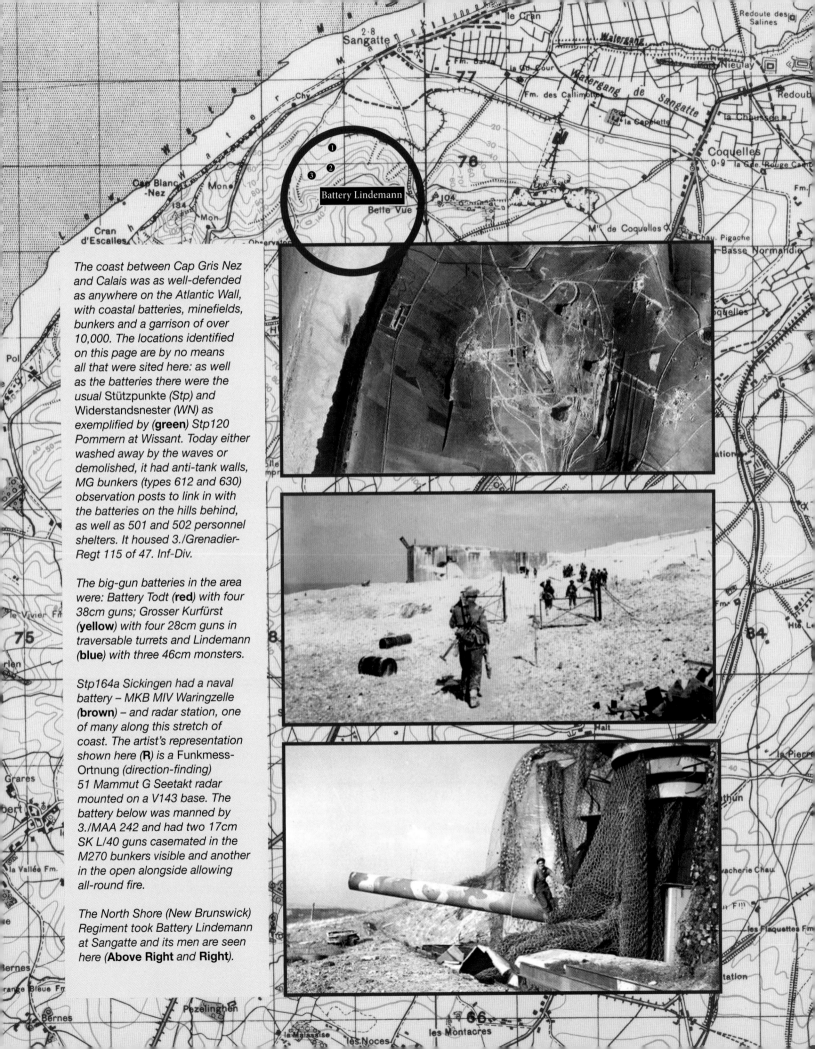

The coast between Cap Gris Nez and Calais was as well-defended as anywhere on the Atlantic Wall, with coastal batteries, minefields, bunkers and a garrison of over 10,000. The locations identified on this page are by no means all that were sited here: as well as the batteries there were the usual Stützpunkte (Stp) and Widerstandsnester (WN) as exemplified by (**green**) Stp120 Pommern at Wissant. Today either washed away by the waves or demolished, it had anti-tank walls, MG bunkers (types 612 and 630) observation posts to link in with the batteries on the hills behind, as well as 501 and 502 personnel shelters. It housed 3./Grenadier-Regt 115 of 47. Inf-Div.

The big-gun batteries in the area were: Battery Todt (**red**) with four 38cm guns; Grosser Kurfürst (**yellow**) with four 28cm guns in traversable turrets and Lindemann (**blue**) with three 46cm monsters.

Stp164a Sickingen had a naval battery – MKB MIV Waringzelle (**brown**) – and radar station, one of many along this stretch of coast. The artist's representation shown here (**R**) is a Funkmess-Ortnung (direction-finding) 51 Mammut G Seetakt radar mounted on a V143 base. The battery below was manned by 3./MAA 242 and had two 17cm SK L/40 guns casemated in the M270 bunkers visible and another in the open alongside allowing all-round fire.

The North Shore (New Brunswick) Regiment took Battery Lindemann at Sangatte and its men are seen here (**Above Right** and **Right**).

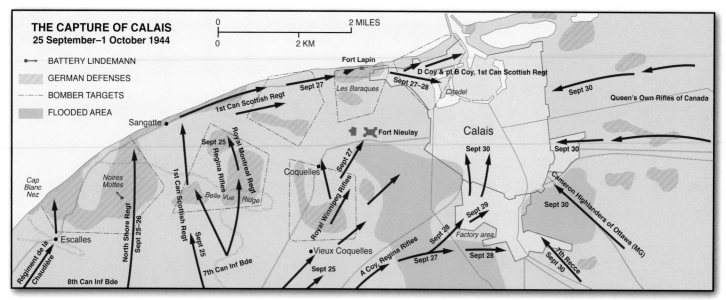

THE CAPTURE OF CALAIS
25 September–1 October 1944

0   2 MILES
0   2 KM

- BATTERY LINDEMANN
- GERMAN DEFENSES
- BOMBER TARGETS
- FLOODED AREA

Fort Lapin

D Coy & pt B Coy, 1st Can Scottish Regt

Sept 27   Les Baraques   Sept 27–28   Citadel   Sept 30

1st Can Scottish Regt   Queen's Own Rifles of Canada

Sangatte

Sept 25   Fort Nieulay   Calais

Royal Montreal Regt   Sept 30

Regina Rifles   Coquelles   Sept 27   Royal Winnipeg Rifles   Sept 30

Cap Blanc Nez   Belle Vue Ridge   Cameron Highlanders of Ottawa (MG)

Noires Mottes   Sept 29

1st Can Scottish Regt   Factory area

Sept 25   Sept 30

Escalles   Sept 25   Vieux Coquelles   A Coy, Regina Rifles   Sept 28   7th Recce   Sept 30

Régiment de la Chaudière   North Shore Regt   Sept 25-26   7th Can Inf Bde   Sept 25   Sept 27   Sept 28

8th Can Inf Bde

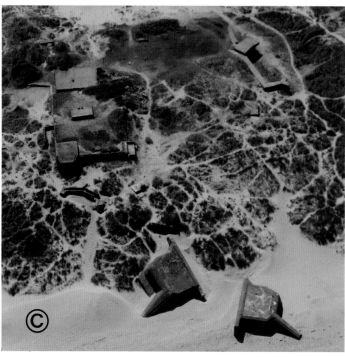

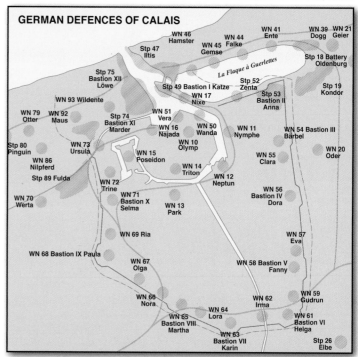

GERMAN DEFENCES OF CALAIS

WN 46 Hamster   WN 44 Falke   WN 41 Ente   WN 39 Dogg   WN 21 Geier

Stp 47 Iltis   WN 45 Gemse

Stp 75 Bastion XII Löwe   Stp 49 Bastion I Katze   Stp 52 Zenta   Stp 53 Bastion II Anna   Stp 18 Battery Oldenburg

La Flaque à Guerlettes   Stp 19 Kondor

WN 93 Wildente   WN 17 Nixe

WN 79 Otter   WN 92 Maus   Stp 74 Bastion XI Marder   WN 51 Vera   WN 50 Wanda   WN 11 Nymphe   WN 54 Bastion III Bärbel

WN 16 Najada   WN 20 Oder

Stp 80 Pinguin   WN 73 Ursula   WN 10 Olymp   WN 55 Clara

WN 86 Nilpferd   WN 15 Poseidon   WN 14 Triton

Stp 89 Fulda   WN 12 Neptun   WN 56 Bastion IV Dora

WN 72 Trine

WN 70 Werta   WN 71 Bastion X Selma   WN 13 Park

WN 69 Ria   WN 57 Eva

WN 68 Bastion IX Paula   WN 58 Bastion V Fanny

WN 67 Olga

WN 66 Nora   WN 62 Irma   WN 59 Gudrun

WN 64 Lora   WN 61 Bastion VI Helga

WN 65 Bastion VIII Martha   WN 63 Bastion VII Karin   Stp 26 Elbe

Ⓒ

Ⓑ

Ⓑ

Opposite:

Above: *Operation Undergo was initially hard-fought, but after Battery Lindemann fell, under cover of a smokescreen further attacks led to wholesale surrender.*

Centre Left: *WN79 Otter – HQ of MAA 244 – is just to the east of Stp 80 Pinguin MKB Fort Lapin and sinking slowly into the sea. Visible are two 612 casemates; behind them a large command post which was tied in to the various batteries— Lindemann, Oldenburg, Todt, and Grosser Kurfürst—in the area.*

Centre Right: *The German strongpoints surrounding Calais.*

Below Left and Right: *Stp 89 Fulda's* Dombunker *– a literal translation is cathedral bunker – was built to protect railway guns. Alongside is a massive ammo store.*

This Page: *Calais looking west. At* **A** *the citadel;* **B** *Stp Fulda's* Dombunker; *C* Stp Otter; *D* Fort Lapin; *E* Cap Blanc Nez.

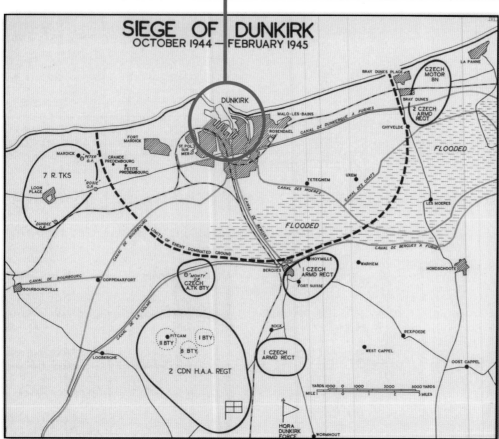

SIEGE OF DUNKIRK
OCTOBER 1944 — FEBRUARY 1945

Left and Below Left: *2nd Can Inf Div arrived on the outskirts of Dunkirk on 7 September. There was heavy fighting up to the 15th, with air support. However, of all the Channel ports, Dunkirk, commanded by Admiral Friedrich Frisius, was best set up for a long defence with a garrison of 10,000 men – including 2,000 Waffen-SS – and the morale necessary to hold the fortress. It also hoped for resupply by sea from the German-held northern Netherlands, although in reality this was sporadic, but included use of the Seehund (seal) two-man submarines. The Allies decided to mask Dunkirk rather than lose men unnecessarily. A number of units were involved initially, and on 3–6 October a truce allowed 17,500 French civilians and wounded soldiers to leave the city. On 9 October the siege was handed over to 1st Czech Armd Bde which spent the rest of the war undertaking aggressive patrols, taking prisoners and having to withstand sallies from the fortress in November 1944. Frisius surrendered on 9 May 1945. This photo (**Left**) shows the bombing of the port earlier in the war.*

Opposite:
Above Left and Right: *Manhandling a 3.7-inch AA gun to be used in the bombardment of Dunkirk. Much of the locality had been flooded (see map) and the conditions during the winter of 1944–45 were extremely nasty as the water table rose.*

Centre Left: *A visit to the eccentric but brilliant Canada-Poland War Museum at Adagem is a must.*

Centre Right: *First to enter Bruges on 12 September was the 12th Manitoba Dragoons, an event commemorated by the bisons flanking Canada Bridge.*

Below: *'Clanky', a Sherman V, remembers the heavy fighting around Eeklo, liberated on 12 September and its suburb Balgerhoeke where the tank is situated. It has been given the markings of C Sqn, South Alberta Regt, 4th Can Armd Div and the name and number of the tank used by the regiment's CO, Maj David Currie, VC.*

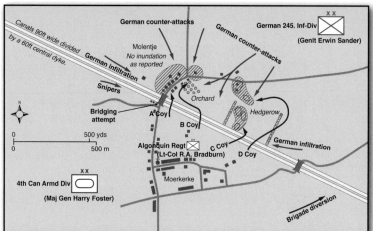

Canals 90ft wide divided by a 60ft central dyke.

German infiltration

German counter-attacks

Molentje
No inundation
as reported

German counter-attacks

German 245. Inf-Div
(Genlt Erwin Sander)

Snipers

Orchard

N

Bridging
attempt

A Coy

B Coy

Hedgerow

German infiltration

0   500 yds
0   500 m

Algonquin Regt
(Lt-Col R.A. Bradburn)

C Coy

D Coy

4th Can Armd Div
(Maj Gen Harry Foster)

Moerkerke

Brigade diversion

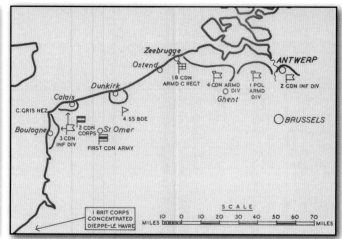

Zeebrugge

Ostend

ANTWERP

Dunkirk

18 CDN
ARMD C REGT

4 CDN ARMD
DIV

I POL
ARMD
DIV

2 CDN INF DIV

C. GRIS NEZ

Calais

Ghent

Boulogne

2 CDN
CORPS

St Omer

4 SS BDE

BRUSSELS

3 CDN
INF DIV

FIRST CDN ARMY

I BRIT CORPS
CONCENTRATED
DIEPPE-LE HAVRE

SCALE

10   0   10   20   30   40   50   60   70
MILES   MILES

Above: *The moment it all went wrong? Late on 13 September the Algonquin Regt gained a slender foothold across the parallel canals at Moerkerke (this –* **Top** *– is the southern of the two, the Dérivation de la Lys known to the Dutch as the Schipdonkcanal). The Germans knew what this meant: Fifteenth Armee's escape over the Scheldt was mid-flow. If the Canadians could break through now there would be serious repercussions. The Germans threw everything at the bridgehead and First Canadian Army had nothing more to support the Algonquins: II Canadian Corps was stretched and I British Corps was too far south (see map* **Above Right** *showing First Canadian Army troop dispositions on 19 September). The many canals in the Low Countries were difficult to cross at the best of times – two in quick succession when opposed were extraordinary difficult. The Algonquins didn't have ferries (as* **Right***) and were instead taken across in 40 assault boats crewed by men of the Lincoln and Welland Regiment. The Allies had at their disposal the versatile Bailey bridge – some 1,500 of which were built between 6 June 1944 and 8 May 1945 – but they were difficult to build under fire and attempts to build a bridge over the canals failed under heavy mortar and artillery fire. The Algonquins had to retreat. They returned by whatever means they could on 14 September, covered by a smokescreen and a heavy artillery barrage, some leaving their kit behind and swimming. Of the original 240 men, there were 134 casualties. The moment passed – the next opportunity didn't arrive for a month.*

1ST POLISH ARMOURED DIVISION

1st Polish Armd Div came under Canadian command in July and was introduced to action for Operation Totalize. It took the right flank on the advance into Belgium and the Netherlands and the Poles are remembered with great fondness by the people they liberated.

Below: *The Poles liberated Tielt in Belgium on 8 September 1944 – a Sherman Firefly Vc commemorates the event. The markings show off the divisional badge and the tactical 53 on a red background indicating the 24th Polish Lancers Regt.*

Above Left: *There isn't much of a welcoming committee, which – knowing the Poles – means they are already in the pub!*

Above Right: *Memorial at Axel in the Netherlands. It remembers 25 soldiers of the division's 10th Dragoons who died here on 17 September. The division helped clear the south bank of the Scheldt to Terneuzen before moving to the east of Antwerp to take part in the drive north.*

Below: *No stopping for the border niceties as the division moves into the Netherlands. Note the tactical triangle on the turret rear and the 53 indicating A Squadron of the 24th Lancers. Having fought in the Dutch territory south of the Scheldt, the Poles had to cross the Dutch border again at Zondereigen on 2 October.*

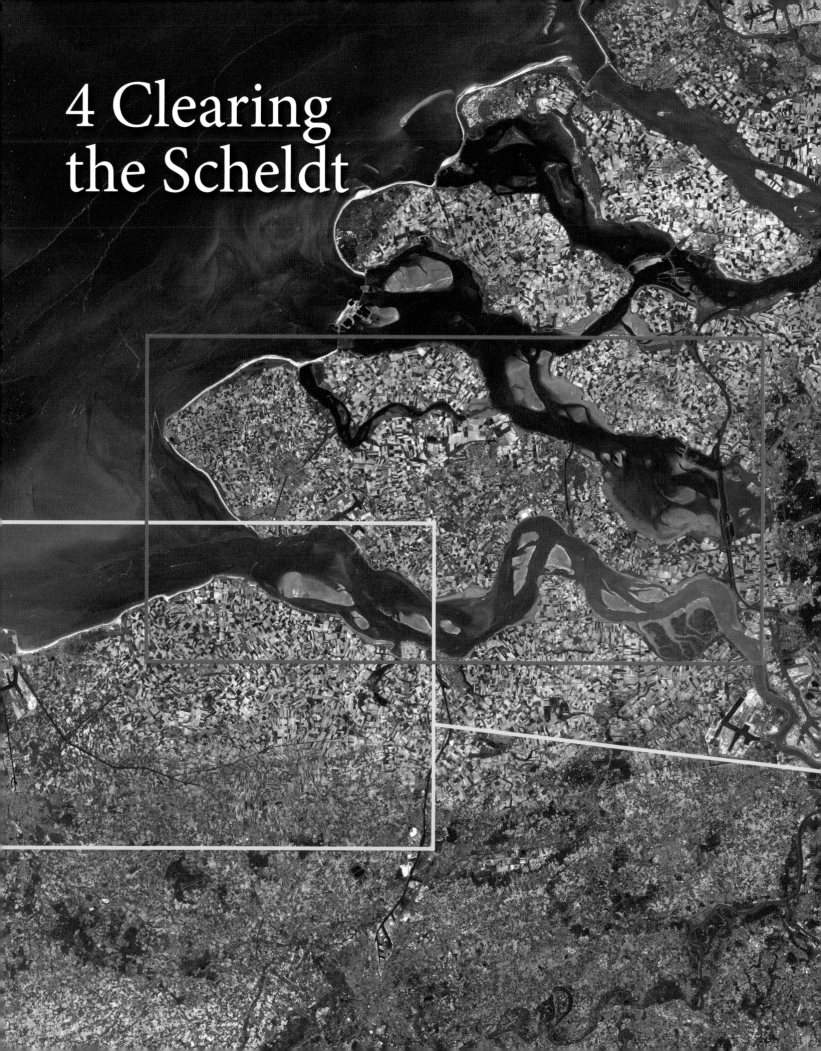

4 Clearing the Scheldt

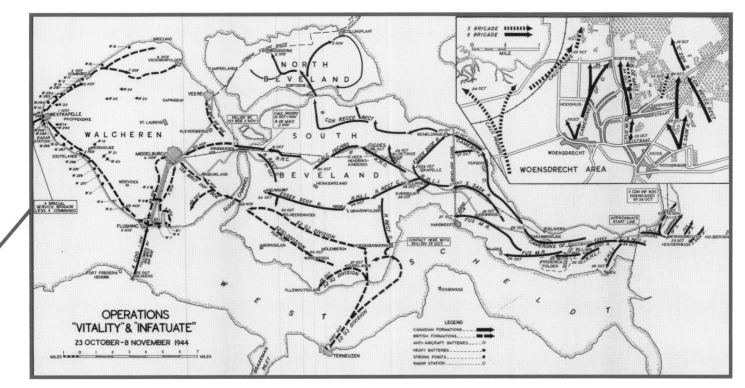

Antwerp became a necessity to relieve the Allies' logistic problems and clearing the estuary fell to First Canadian Army. It was an onerous task that would see hard fighting against a resilient enemy, awful conditions and high casualty rates. This satellite photo shows how much has changed since 1944: land reclamation, new roads, bridges and tunnels have joined Walcheren and Beveland firmly to the Dutch mainland. The contemporary maps show a more difficult landscape of narrow causeways and inundated low ground. Note the location of Moerkerke (**A**) where the Algonquins had crossed the canals on 13 September.

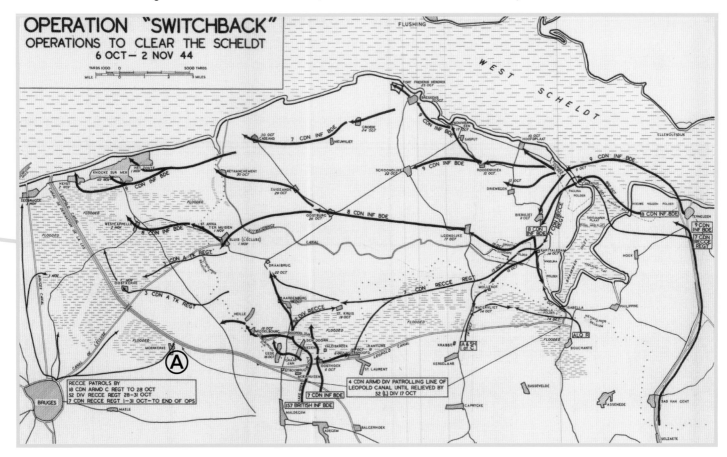

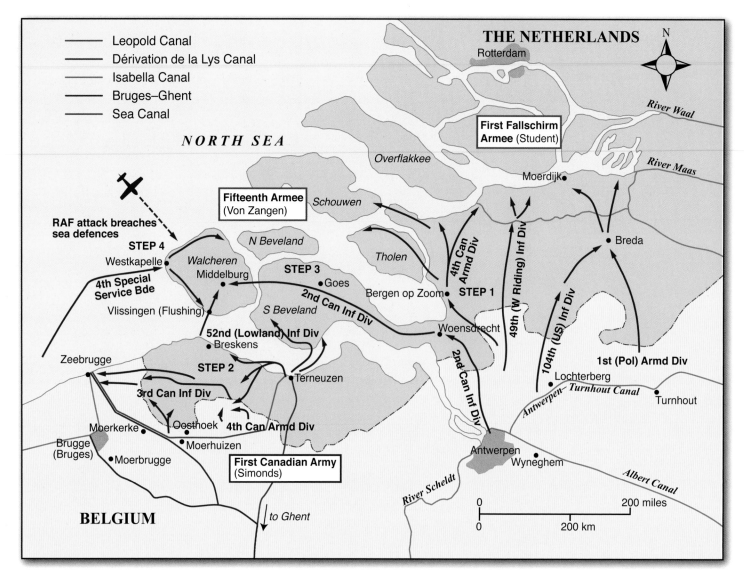

Held at Moerkerke, the Canadian advance stalled as Operation Market Garden dominated September, taking munitions and attention away from the Scheldt. The men of Fifteenth Armee who had crossed over to Walcheren were able to make their way east and play an important role in helping the Germans stop the Allied attack. The failure to bounce the Rhine, outflank the Westwall and defeat Germany in 1944 left the Allies with no choice but the long haul and for that, it became imperative to open the Scheldt to shipping.

It's facile, however, to blame the debacle at Arnhem on Fifteenth Armee's escape across the Scheldt or to assume that an earlier attack on the positions around the Scheldt would have led to a dramatically less costly and speedier result than what actually happened. Truth is, the Allied forces were overstretched after their advance from Normandy. Autumn was cold and wet and the German defence – thanks to units like Kampfgruppe Chill – had thickened enough to stop the collapse. By doing so they extended the war and contributed to many more German deaths as the Allies consolidated, sorted out their supply lines and prepared for a broad-front assault on Germany.

Montgomery had – he admitted it himself – thought clearing the Scheldt would be straightforward. When the blinkers came off in mid-October – thanks to a full and frank exchange with Eisenhower around 15 October – so the weight of Second British Army was applied to the problem. The resulting operations, Pheasant and Suitcase, saw British and Canadian forces push north to the Maas. As part of I Corps the 104th (US) Inf Div reached the river on 5 November.

To the south, First Canadian Army cleared the Breskens Pocket and then the muddy polders of South Beveland. The final operations saw seaborne assaults on 1 November on Walcheren – Infatuate I (Vlissingen), and II (Westkapelle) – leading to a week of intense fighting before the surrender on 8 November. During the Scheldt battles First Canadian Army netted 40,000 PoWs.

But those battles had cost the army dearly: 12,873 men (703 officers and 12,170 ORs) killed, wounded, or lost in action presumed dead. Of these half were Canadian, the other half made up of many nationalities including British, Poles, Americans, Belgians and Norwegians (the latter from No 10 Inter-Allied Commando).

Opposite: *The clearance of the Scheldt was achieved in four hard-won steps by First Canadian Army under the command of Lt Gen Guy Simonds – Crerar having had to return to the UK through illness on 27 September. First, the advance north by 2nd Can Inf Div from Antwerp to Woensdrecht – to close off the Beveland causeway – and further north to close off the avenues of reinforcement and retreat. Step 2 saw 3rd Can Inf Div clear the Breskens Pocket – the south bank of the Scheldt – in Operation Switchback. In Step 3 2nd Can and 52nd (BR) Inf Divs advanced through South Beveland towards Walcheren (Operation Vitality). The final Step 4 was Festung Walcheren itself, an island with deadly concentrations of integrated bunkers and artillery batteries – Operation Infatuate. Once accomplished, these steps successfully disposed of the enemy concentrations, but the Scheldt itself had to be cleared of mines and obstructions – a major undertaking.*

Right: *British troops advance into Antwerp. Elements of XXX Corps first arrived in the city on 4 September. There they were aided by the Belgian resistance.*

Below: *Clearing the Scheldt of mines couldn't start in earnest until the batteries at the mouth of the estuary were neutralised – although the naval forces tried. From 2 November, under gunfire and sometimes in awful weather, the minesweepers did their job. By 26 November, the river had been cleared. There were still casualties: mines were found into December and others were dropped by aircraft and submarine for some time to come. Nevertheless, the port was working just in time to help sustain the Allies during the Battle of the Bulge which began a few weeks later.*

Right: *Step 1. The advance
north started in earnest at the
end of September after the
British 49th (West Riding) Inf
Div established a bridgehead
over the Antwerp–Turnhout
Canal at Lock 7 near
Rijkevorsel on the 25th. 5th Can
Inf Bde crossed on the 28th,
pushing west and clearing the
way for 6th Bde to advance,
joined from Antwerp by the
4th Can Inf Bde. By 8 October
they had reached Hoogerheide.
The German reaction saw the
injection of reinforcements
– 2,000 Fallschirmjäger from
Kampfgruppe Chill trucked
across via Tilburg and Breda –
who counter-attacked on the
9th. This Kampfgruppe was
made up of a number of units,
including the tried and tested
men of FJR6 commanded by
Oberstleutnant (Lt-Col)
Freiherr Friedrich von der
Heydte who had fought the
Americans on D-Day around
Carentan. The Canadian
defensive effort held them off
but attempts to cut the rail and
road link to the peninsula
failed on 'Black Friday' –
13 October – when the Black
Watch of Canada was bloodily
repulsed north of Woensdrecht
(see map on p116). Part of the
town was taken on the 16th
by the Rileys (RHLI) supported by the Fort Garry Horse
but they were halted by the
Fallschirmjäger backed up by
Sturmgeschütz-Brigade-280
(StuG-Bde-280). The advance
was kick-started by Operation
Suitcase on 20 October when
I British Corps with 4th Can
and 1st Polish Armd Divs,
British 49th (West Riding) Inf
Div and – from 23 October
– 104th (US) Inf Div pushed
north. Second British Army
attacked from the east on
22 October.*

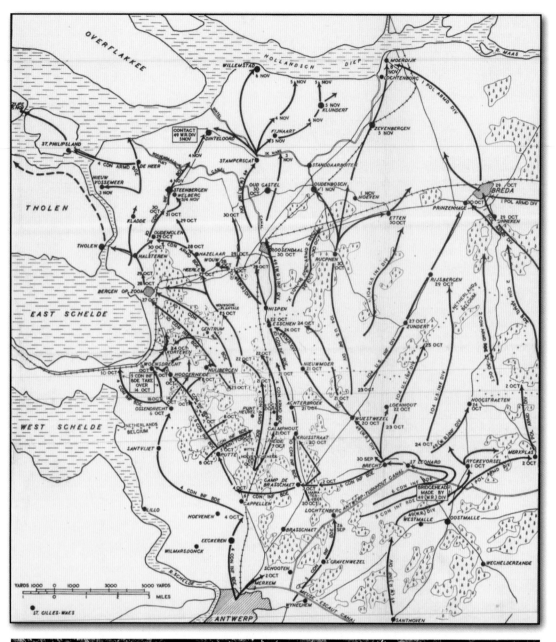

Opposite, Below: *The Monument of Gratitude at Heide station remembers the meeting of Lt-Col Denis Whitaker (RHLI) and Eugene Colson whose resistance fighters had taken and defended Antwerp docks.*

Above: *Woensdrecht was the pivotal location that commanded the entrance to the South Beveland peninsula. This M4A1 in the markings of the Fort Garry Horse has two nearby dedications: one to the Black Watch (Royal Highland Regiment) of Canada 'who fought in the battle for Woensdrecht on Friday, October 13th, 1944 (Black Friday) suffering 183 casualties.' The other is 'In memory of the gallant men of the Royal Hamilton Light Infantry, 2nd Canadian Division. On Oct 16, 1944, they attacked and captured the town of Woensdrecht. Eventually this enabled the Allies to advance to the island of Walcheren and open the port of Antwerp. The RHLI held its objective, enduring intensive fighting and relentless counter-attacks by battle-wise German paratroopers. The price paid was 167 casualties, 21 of them fatal.' It's worth noting that some of the 'battle-wise' paratroopers were anything but that: a good number had only just reached the front, were young and not particularly well-trained. However, there was a core of von der Heydte's veteran FJR6 who held up the Canadian troops. It wasn't until 24 October that Woensdrecht was completely in Canadian hands. Note the bridging classification (30 in yellow circle) on the hull front. This tank was a vehicle supplied to the Royal Netherlands Army postwar by the US Mutual Defense Assistance Act and was retrieved from later use as a range target.*

Right: *A corporal of Le Régiment de Maisonneuve examining a disabled Sturmhaubitze 42 of StuG-Bde-280 on Antwerpsestraatweg, near Woens-drecht, 27 October. Note the 105mm main gun.*

BERGEN-OP-ZOOM

An ancient city – one of the Netherlands' oldest – that has been fought over many times, during the battles around Woensdrecht, Bergen (**A**) had been used as an HQ by the Germansand had also seen civilians flock to it to get away from the fighting. 2nd Can Inf Div had borne the brunt of the advance towards Bergen, but it would be the Lincoln and Welland Regiment, part of 4th Can Armd Div's 10th Inf Bde, that liberated the city. Having moved from the Breskens Pocket area north of Antwerp between 16 and 20 October, the Lincs and the Algonquins took Esschen on the 22nd. Hard fighting around the village of Wouwsche (taken on the 25th with over 300 casualties) delayed the attack on Bergen to 27 October. Inside the city, von der Heydte had made a momentous decision – partly forced on him by the sheer number of civilians there – to abandon the city. It was one of the last command decisions he made, having been ordered away to run a training school for Fallschirmjäger officers in Aalten. Having spent the 26th and 27th clearing the town of anything of military advantage to the Allies (including church spires), the Germans left Bergen. The Lincoln and Welland supported by the South Alberta Regt (seen **Below**) were soon in the main square. Note **B** the railway line to Walcheren where the Black Watch of Canada attacked on 13 October and **C** the suburbs of Woensdrecht. The map shows overlays of German defences.

This Page: *The 1st Polish Armd Div played an important role in the advance north. It crossed the Antwerp–Turnhout Canal on 28 September and immediately was involved in heavy fighting. It advanced slowly, held up south of Tilburg by Kampfgruppe Chill before moving northwest to attack Breda which it reached on 29 October. As was the case in a number of the attacks on Dutch cities, the Allies refrained as far as possible from the use of artillery and bombing to keep down civilian casualties – something they had been unable to do in France. Unfortunately, this wasn't often the case and many thousands of civilians died in bombardments. In Breda, however, Maczek's attack from the east took the Germans by surprise and the city fell to the 3rd (Pol) Inf Bde without the drawn-out house-to-house fighting that took place elsewhere. To commemorate the victory, postwar the Poles presented the city with a PzKpfw V Panther Ausf D (**Below**) which was painted to its current standard in 2004. 1st Polish Armd Div continued to press northwards, reaching Moerdijk where it spent the winter.*

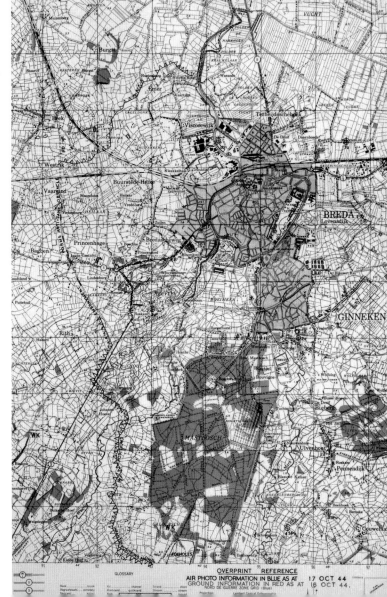

MAIN BRITISH AND CANADIAN OPERATIONS IN AUTUMN 1944

Operation	Start	Mission
Market Garden	17.09	Attempt to outflank the Westwall
Switchback	06.10	Clearing the Breskens Pocket
Suitcase	20.10	Canadian First Army pushes north from Antwerp area to secure S Beveland causeway
Pheasant	22.10	Second British Army attacks west from Eindhoven salient to clear North Brabant, the area south of the River Maas
Vitality I	23.10	Clearing South Beveland for the attack on Walcheren island from the causeway
Vitality II	23.10	Amphibious attack by 52nd (Lowland) Division on South Beveland
Infatuate I	01.11	Amphibious attack on Vlissingen (Flushing), Walcheren
Infatuate II	01.11	Amphibious attack on Westkapelle, Walcheren

Above Left: *The 4th Can Armd Div was involved initially in the fighting to cross the Bruges–Ghent Canal at Moerbrugge, where this memorial to the South Alberta Regt – the division's recce unit – stands. It then patrolled on the Leopold Canal until sent north of Antwerp.*

Left: *Visit of General Dwight Eisenhower to 4th Can Armd Div on 29 November after the fighting to clear the Scheldt had been completed.*

Below: *It wasn't often that First Canadian Army had US troops under command. The 104th (US) Infantry Division were unblooded when they entered action on 23 October 1944. They had arrived in France on 7 September assigned to III Corps of Ninth (US) Army. Under the charismatic Terry Allen, dismissed from command of 1st (US) Infantry after personality clashes with Bradley and Patton, the 'Timberwolves' hit the ground running, supporting I British Corps' advance north. In two weeks of action they advanced to the Maas, liberating Zundert (where this memorial is placed) on the way. The weather was awful and the casualties high – 1,426 including 313 dead.*

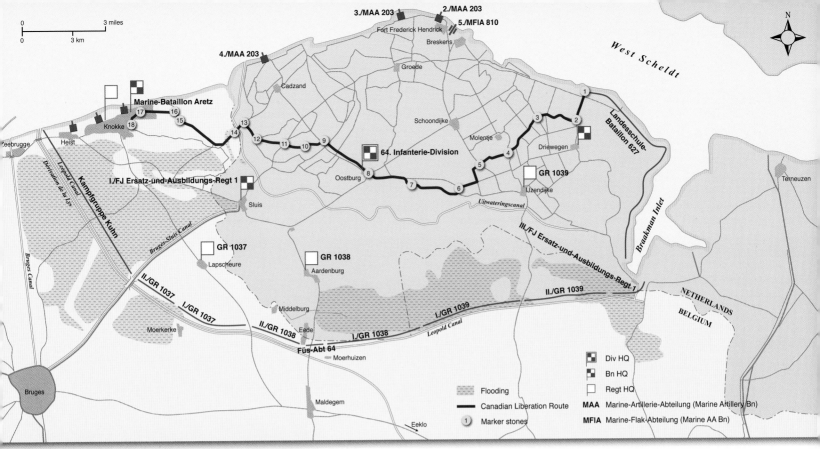

The German forces in the Breskens Pocket.

Above: *The German forces in the Breskens Pocket. Step 2 in the clearance of the Scheldt started on 6 October – against strong opposition from German 64. Inf-Div, whose commander, Generalmajor Knut Eberding, had over 11,000 men ranged against Operation Switchback were there for the long term – those elements of the German Fifteenth Armee that were going to leave had left. The Breskens Pocket and Walcheren were fortresses designed to control the Scheldt and had bunkers and batteries aplenty. It took considerable effort and many lives before they surrendered. This map also shows the Canadian Liberation Route that is walked every year to remember those who died. It starts at Hoofdplaat (1) where part of 9th Can Inf Bde's amphibious landing took place on 6 October, and ends at Knokke (18) which fell on 3 November.*

Left: *The development of the Ronson flame system in Canada led to the Wasp – a Universal Carrier equipped with a flamethrower. This is a training version with twin tanks. The in-service model used by the Canadian Army was the IIC with one external tank. Used in carrier platoons, they entered service in late 1944 – before then Crocodiles (mainly Churchills) were used. 27 Wasps helped start the attack by 7th Can Inf Bde over the Leopold Canal.*

Below: *RCA 5.5-inch gun in operation. There were over 300 guns ready for use during Operation Switchback from the super-heavy 240mm and 8in guns of 9 (BR) AGRA to the 144 25pdrs of 3rd Can Inf and 4th Can Armd Divs. German 64. Inf-Div had around 70 guns of 75mm or larger, including the assets of MAA 203 and 204. Walcheren was also close enough to take part in artillery bombardments.*

The plan (see map p111) for Operation Switchback was for 7th Can Inf Bde to attack from the south near Oosthoek on 6 October and 8th Bde to push through once an opening had been made. 9th Bde would make an amphibious landing on the north coast on the 8th, launching from Terneuzen which had been taken on 20 September by 1st Polish Armd Div. Things did not go quite to plan. The initial attack across the Leopold Canal – supported by Wasps – provided two small bridgeheads which could not link up because of heavy artillery fire and counter-attacks. However, although delayed by a day, the amphibious attack when it went through on the 9th was entirely successful. The same day the bridgeheads across the canal linked up and Bailey bridges were pushed over. (**Left** An example, the Oosthoekbrug, is preserved.) The fighting was still intense on the flooded polders, but on the 14th attacks from the east by the 10th Can Inf Bde (of 4th Can Armd Div) – the Algonquins and Argyll and Sutherland Highlanders of Canada – made some progress and in the south, on the 18th, the British 52nd (Lowland) Inf Div – by some army irony specialist mountain troops – took over the positions of the 7th Bde, the 8th having been transferred through Terneuzen to support the 9th. Eede was liberated on the 16th and by the time the 9th Bde and Lowlanders met up on the 19th, half the pocket had been taken along with 3,000 PoWs. Unfortunately, this did not deter the Germans who, supported by reinforcements from Walcheren along with fire from the coastal batteries, continued to fight for every inch of ground. Nevertheless, Breskens fell on 22 October, Fort Frederick Hendrick surrendered on the 24th, Oostburg on the 26th, Retranchement the 30th, Knokke by 2 November and Zeebrugge by the 3rd.

Opposite, Below Left: *Lt-Col D.G. Crofton of the Canadian Scottish Regt looks over what's left of a German 15.5cm gun near Breskens, 28 October. Note beach defences.*

Opposite, Centre Right: *A memorial at Eede remembers the Canadian forces involved in the pocket. It's also the Dutch national memorial to the return from exile of Queen Wilhelmina of the Netherlands on May 1945.*

Opposite, Below Right: *On 20 October an incident at IJzendijke involving mine-clearing Congas, which used nitroglycerine, led to an explosion that knocked out a number of vehicles and killed 41 men – 27 of them were from 284 Armd Assault Sqn, RE (from 79th Armd Div), 10 RCASC, 3 from 11th Essex Regt, RA and 1 REME. This memorial was erected in 1997.*

Above: *On the Liberation Route, this is the Hickmanbrug memorial. 'At the end of October 1944, the Royal Canadian Engineer Regiment, under the leadership of Sgt J.L. Hickman, reached the drainage canal at Retranchement. Under heavy shell fire, they erected a Bailey bridge on this site on 31 October 1944, where Sgt Hickman was mortally wounded.' The Canadian troops were advancing towards Zeebrugge – to the left of this photo.*

Above Right: *Memorial to the 12th Manitoba Dragoons who liberated the port of Zeebrugge on 3 November 1944.*

Right: *The 4th Can Armd Div captured this 17cm railway gun of Batterie 718 (it had three) near Knokke on 13 October. The Germans had a great deal of artillery around the Scheldt some of which – such as the 15cm coastal guns at Walcheren – had a range of 14 miles.*

Step 3 in the battle of the Scheldt was Operation Vitality – clearing South Beveland. With Woensdrecht in Allied hands, 2nd Can Inf Div was ready to go on 24 October. It took three days to reach the South Beveland Canal that split the island and held up the attack – but the day before, elements of the British 52nd (Lowland) Inf Div assaulted the south of the island from Terneuzen in Operation Vitality II. They were transported in 137 Buffaloes to make the journey. Helped by a bombardment from Ossenisse, the Lowlanders' 156th Inf Bde – 4th and 5th Bns, Royal Scots Fusiliers and 6th Cameronians – landed on two beaches, one of which proved unusable. Baarland was quickly captured and reinforcements arrived, including 18 Shermans and the 7th Cameronians. With their canal line position flanked the Germans retreated to Walcheren and by the 30th South Beveland was liberated. The Allies stood at the end of the Walcheren Causeway.

Above Left: *The Lowlanders prepare to leave.*

Left and Below Left: *Memorial and info board on Amber Beach, where the 52nd Division landed.*

Below: *Sherman Ic Firefly of the Fort Garry Horse nearing the South Beveland Canal on 29 October.*

Above and Below: *On 27 October men of the Rileys move through Krabbendijke – which had been liberated the day before – towards Walcheren, using carriers (**Above**) and GM C15TA armoured trucks (**Below**).*

Above and Below Right: *Step 4 was Walcheren. The causeway over was a frightening prospect – half a mile long and less than 100yd wide. At the other end, the opposition had ranged weapons – the mortars were particularly deadly. It was important that the attack over the causeway took place as soon as possible because at the other side of the island two amphibious landings were planned, at Vlissingen and Westkapelle – Infatuate I and II respectively. The causeway battle was supposed to draw the*

German response away from the western operations. The Black Watch of Canada attacked on 1 November, followed later that night by the Calgary Highlanders who managed to fight their way to a small bridgehead. This was counter-attacked strongly and pushed back before being re-established by Le Régiment de Maisonneuve who then handed over to the British Lowland Division, elements of which had crossed the Sloe Channel between Walcheren and South Beveland on the 2nd. Linkup was achieved on the 5th and the division fought its way to Middelburg where the commander of the island fortress, Genlt Wilhelm Daser of 70. Inf-Div, surrendered on 6 November. A month later, the Antwerp docks were open for business and the men of First Canadian Army entered a three-month period of relative calm along the River Maas.

Attacked from three locations – the causeway and by two amphibious operations – German troops (mainly 70. Inf-Div) on Walcheren resisted for a week. The landings at Westkapelle on 1 November were heavily opposed and both the landing force and the naval component took a battering – 172 killed and 125 wounded from the courageous RN Support Group alone. It had 16 of its 27 craft put out of action while engaging the key W13 and W15 batteries (**A** and **B** on map). Naval gunfire and timely assistance from RAF Typhoons helped the troops get ashore. Note use of Buffaloes launched from LCTs (**Above**) heading towards White Beach, one of two used for the attack. The other was Red; Green Beach was used later for supplies.

Above and Centre Right: *The Commando attack on Westkapelle.*

Below Right: *Memorial at Westkapelle. This Sherman V was a flail tank of the 1st Lothians and Border Horse, one of the 79th Armd Div's 'Funnies' that landed on 1 November but was flooded.*

Opposite, Above: *RAF bombing had opened the dykes and flooded the interior of Walcheren rendering much of the defence infrastructure unusable, but also concentrating the attackers on the better defended dykes. The bombing wasn't discussed with the Dutch Government-in-Exile, caused huge damage to the land (the dykes weren't restored until October 1945 and draining the island continued well into 1946), death of livestock (only 600 cows survived out of nearly 10,000) and destruction of buildings.*

Opposite, Centre and Below Left: *The inundation. Note lighthouse at **C**.*

Opposite, Right: *Contemporary map showing German defences. The 70. Inf-Div that defended Walcheren was one of the so-called 'stomach' divisions made up of men who would normally have been unfit for duty. They were grouped together to make diet and medication easier to deal with. They weren't, however, first class troops.*

HOLLAND 1:5000 **DEFENCE OVERPRINT** EDITION OF 25 OCT. 44 **TOWN OF WESTKAPELLE**

THE BATTERIES

A = W13 (7./MAA 202): 4 x 15cm, 2 x 7.5cm for close defence, 3 x 2cm AA. Ran out of ammo 10:17.

B = W15 (6./MAA 202): 4 x 3.7-inch, 2 x 3-inch for close defence (both types ex-BR captured at Dunkirk). KO'd by HMS *Roberts*, air and ground attack by 12:15.

RED beach

WHITE beach

WESTKAPELLE

FLOODED AT HIGH TIDE

GREEN beach

REFER TO THIS MAP AS —
HOLLAND 1:5000
CA 15 SHEET NO.I
DEFENCE OVERPRINT
25 OCT 44

OVERPRINT REFERENCE
AIR PHOTO INFORMATION AS AT 21 OCT 44
GROUND INFORMATION (G.S.) AS AT 21 OCT 44

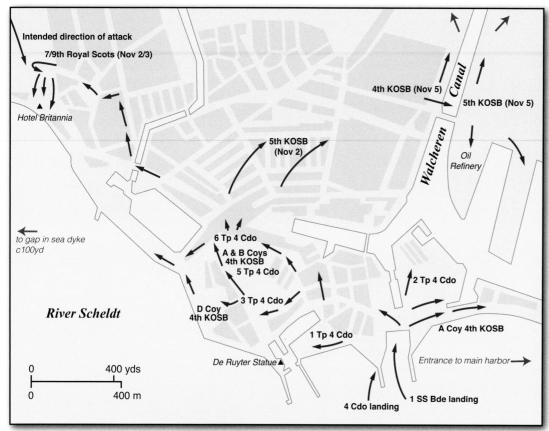

Intended direction of attack

7/9th Royal Scots (Nov 2/3)

Hotel Britannia

4th KOSB (Nov 5)

5th KOSB (Nov 5)

Walcheren Canal

Oil Refinery

5th KOSB (Nov 2)

to gap in sea dyke c100yd

6 Tp 4 Cdo

A & B Coys 4th KOSB

5 Tp 4 Cdo

2 Tp 4 Cdo

River Scheldt

3 Tp 4 Cdo

D Coy 4th KOSB

A Coy 4th KOSB

1 Tp 4 Cdo

0	400 yds
0	400 m

De Ruyter Statue ▲

Entrance to main harbor →

4 Cdo landing

1 SS Bde landing

Left: *Vlissingen was assaulted by No 4 Cdo with follow-up troops from 155th (BR) Inf Bde (4th and 5th Bns, KOSB and 7th/9th Royal Scots). Counter-battery fire from Breskens helped and the British troops soon made their way through the town before getting held up by the many strongpoints in the direction of Middelburg. Negotiating their way around by using Buffaloes and guided by the resistance, the troops made their way into Middelburg where they accepted the surrender of the German forces.*

Below Left: *Memorial on the quayside at Vlissingen to No 4 Cdo and the citizens of the town who died during the war.*

Below: *Canadian First Army used a new weapon during the attack on Vlissingen. Codenamed Land Mattress (the naval version had been used at D-Day from LCT(R)s), its success under 112th Bty of 6th LAA Regt, RCA led to the creation of the 1st Canadian Rocket Bty. They fired 1,000 of the rockets, each armed with a 7lb warhead, in six hours. Here it's being tested at Helchteren, Belgium, on 29 October.*

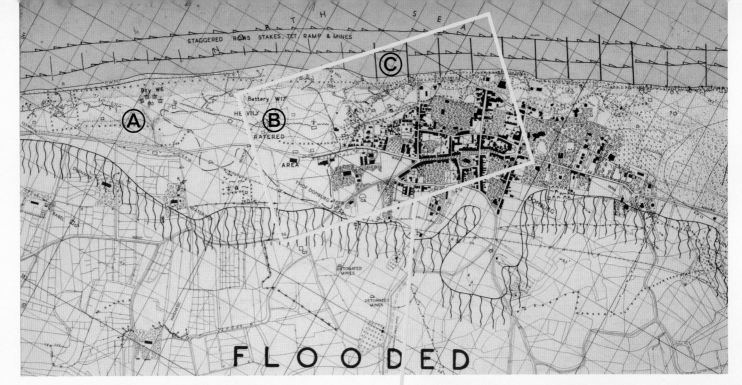

FLOODED

DOMBURG

Some four miles from Vlissingen, Domburg was the location of three batteries: **A** W5 with 4 x AA 9.4cm guns; **B** W17 (5./MAA 202) of four 22cm guns with one 5cm gun for close support; **C** W37 with 4 x 15cm guns integrated into Stp Swinemunde (west) and Stp Zoppot. This area was assaulted by Nos 41 and 10(IA) Cdos from Westkapelle after neutralising W15. After having taken Domburg they pressed on to clear the northeast corner of the island along with No 4 Cdo. There are memorials to the Belgian and Norwegian elements of No 10(IA) at Domburg.

The opening of the Scheldt saw the First Canadian Army enter a period of relative calm as it spent its winter on the banks of the Maas. This is not to say that the time was without incident: on 16 December Hitler unleashed a substantial surprise attack in the Ardennes that caught the Allies napping. For a short while the German spearheads threatened the Meuse bridges, but as soon as the weather improved, Allied airpower took its toll and the Germans retreated. The Canadian involvement was more about being in a position to respond rather than responding, although 1st Can Para Bn was involved as part of British 6th Airborne Division.

The war had entered a difficult period for the British and Canadian forces. They had been fighting for five years and were short of infantrymen. For the Canadians this was a political hot potato not always helped by periods of leave. When men who

had been fighting for so long saw the number of men who had not seen action and refused to serve abroad, there was bad feeling. Added to this, the units at the front wanted their veterans back, not greenhorns. The immediate problems were alleviated by a cunning plan. Operation Goldflake moved I Canadian Corps and 5th (BR) Inf Div in secret from Italy to northwest Europe. Between the end of February and the end of April over 60,000 troops made the journey complete with trucks and tanks.

They arrived just in time. Monty's long-awaited Operation Veritable stuttered while it awaited the start of the American Operation Grenade – held up because the dams holding back the Roer hadn't been captured allowing the Germans once more to use flooding to hold the Allies up. First Canadian Army – back under Crerar's command – was in the forefront as Hitler made what the 21st Army Group

Opposite: *Sherman tanks of HQ Sqn, British Columbia Regiment (Duke of Connaught's Own), taking on more ammunition after shelling a German position near Meppen, Germany, 8 April. The regiment's tactical sign would have been a blue triangle as it was the junior regiment in the 4th Armd Bde.*

Right: *Opening the Scheldt meant that the Allies' critical supply shortages were soon a thing of the past. More of a problem – to British and Canadian armies – was a manpower shortage, particularly of infantrymen. Operation Goldflake considerably eased First Canadian Army's problems.*

Below: *Canadian First Army at the start of 1945.*

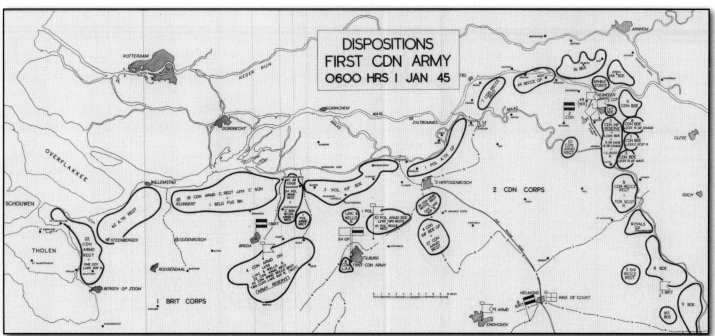

commander felt was his third major strategic blunder – the first, fighting on in Normandy rather than falling back to the Seine; the second was counter-attacking in the Ardennes; this, third, mistake was to allow what forces Germany had to fight west of the Rhine and get involved in a slugging match from which, as more and more American divisions arrived in theatre, was only going to end one way: annihilation. The Allies crossed the Rhine, broke the final defences and then advanced almost at will through Germany, the Netherlands, Austria and even Czechoslovakia.

This is not to say that the fighting got any easier. Wherever the Canadians advanced there always seemed to be the best Germany could offer in front of them – usually Fallschirmjäger – and there were bitter battles on every front until the surrender on 8 May.

Above Left: *Typical Dutch conditions – German machine guns on the dykes raking inundated muddy fields that were difficult enough to negotiate without enemy fire.*

Centre Left: *The flat lands of the Low Countries were perfect for the 8.8cm which could engage targets before they could get near enough to respond.*

Left: *21st Army Group operations in 1945.*
- *Veritable/Blockbuster (8 Feb–11 March) cleared the western bank of the Rhine, fighting through the Reichswald.*
- *Plunder (23–27 March) was the Rhine crossing. (See pp136–140.)*
- *Varsity (24 March) was the airborne side of Plunder. (See p138.)*
- *Destroyer (2–3 April) cleared the Island. (See p145.)*
- *Cannonshot (11 April) crossed the IJssel at Gorssel and attacked west towards Apeldoorn.(See pp146–147.)*
- *Anger (12–16 April) liberated Arnhem. (See p148.)*
- *Cleanser (15–18 April) liberated the area north of Arnhem to the IJsselmeer. (See p149.)*

Allied operations on the Lower Rhine, 8 February–15 April 1945

1. VERITABLE/BLOCKBUSTER
2. PLUNDER
3. VARSITY
4. DESTROYER
5. CANNONSHOT
6. ANGER
7. CLEANSER

THE NETHERLANDS

GERMANY

KAPELSCHE VEER

There are a lot of waterways in the central Netherlands as the three major rivers of the area – the Maas (Meuse in French), Waal and Nederrijn – head to the sea, and a lot of islands. The Kapelsche Veer in the Maas is one of them, flat and featureless, and if anything points to the sheer perversity of fighting at this stage of the war it's the battles fought between I British Corps and German 6. Fallschirmjäger-Division who were well dug in on the island. Worried that it could form the base for an attack over the Maas, which might have made life difficult for the Allies during the Ardennes offensive, Lt Gen Sir John Croker ordered it should be taken. Between 31 December when the Poles made the first attack and 31 January when the Germans finally abandoned it, there were numerous attacks and around 1,000 casualties. Included in the final attack – Operation Elephant conducted by the 4th Can Armd Div with full artillery and tank assistance – was a canoe party of the Lincs that was hampered by ice and forced to land. The final inch-by-inch assault by the Lincs in the west and Argylls in the east took four days and the Canadians sustained 234 casualties including 65 dead.

Above Right: *Polish Shermans on the Kapelsche Veer.*

Centre Right: *Men of the Lincs – the Lincoln and Welland Regiment – practise for a canoe infiltration. (See also p141.)*

Right: *The memorial has panels for the units that took part: 1st Pol Armd Div, No 47 Cdo, 5 Tp (Norwegian) No 10(IA) Cdo, Lincoln and Welland Regiment, Argyll and Sutherland Highlanders of Canada, South Alberta Regiment, Algonquin Regiment, New Brunswick Rangers and Brigade Piron (for a later incident).*

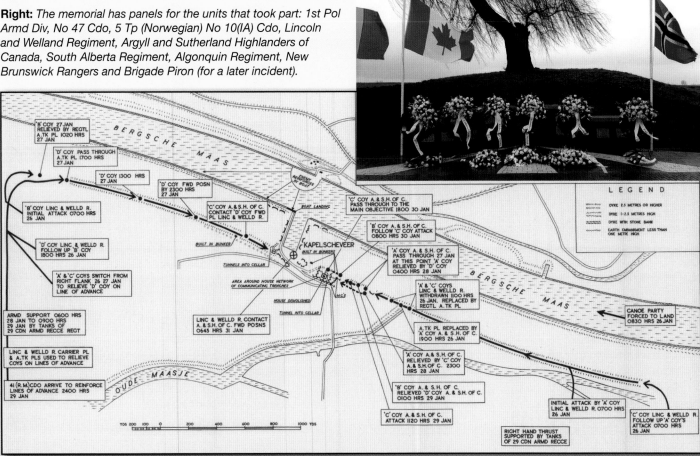

BATTLE OF THE BULGE

Yes, there was a Canadian involvement, when – as part of British 6th Airborne Division's 3rd Para Bde – 1st Can Para Bn was sent to Rochefort in Belgium in late December. Unhappy at having to travel by sea and road rather than their usual air transport (a para-drop was called off because of bad weather), they arrived without adequate cold-weather clothing and footwear and spent two uncomfortable weeks patrolling the area. While on patrol, one unit found direct evidence in Bande – in the form of 34 dead young men – of civilians murdered by German SD troops who had been sent there deliberately to 'retaliate' for the death of three soldiers at the hands of the Belgian resistance on 5 September 1944. It was their last involvement in the Ardennes after which they pulled out and moved to the Netherlands where they stayed until late February 1945 when they returned to England to prepare for their final parachute drop of the war: Operation Varsity.

Left: *Canadian paras in Bande, January 1945. Note the wooden-stocked Sten Mk V carried by the sergeant at left.*

While Second British Army sat on the Maas opposite Venlo (there were plans for Operation Veritable to include a thrust from here), First Canadian Army began the battle to clear the German forces from the northern Rhineland on 8 February 1945. Under command was British XXX Corps which would lead the initial attack which included 2nd and 3rd Can Inf Divs.

The buildup to the operation was huge and carried out carefully and secretively in order to keep the Germans guessing. While it was impossible for the final stages to go unremarked, it's interesting to note that the top Germans – OB West GFM Gerd von Rundstedt and the commander of Heeresgruppe H, Generaloberst Johannes Blaskowitz – both thought Venlo was the likely main attack point.

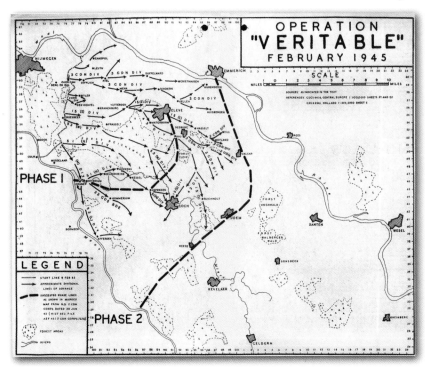

Opposite, Below Right: *The conditions were difficult. The Canadian official history noted that 'the principal obstacle was mud. Routes soon became churned up by the armour; in some cases the axes of advance became impassable to all but infantry and the lightest of vehicles.' Tanks got easily bogged but, if lucky, they could be recovered by another tank – as here with a Sherman of the South Alberta Regiment, Louisendorf, Germany, 26 February 1945.*

Left: *The preparations for Veritable were substantial. New roads were constructed to ease traffic through the muddy and boggy landscape. Here, personnel of the RCE rebuild a corduroy road to maintain the flow of supplies forward.*

Centre Left: *Gunners of a medium regiment fuse 5.5-inch shells near Nijmegen. The weight of the bombardment at the start of Veritable included the artillery of seven divisions and five AGRAs. On top of this were the bombers of RAF Bomber Command and the tactical support of 2TAF.*

Below: *Infantrymen of 1st Bn, Canadian Scottish Regiment, firing three-inch mortars at German positions on 8 February. Any shortages of ammunition had been sorted out over winter.*

Right: *This memorial at Groesbeek is double-sided – one remembers Operation Veritable (this side); on the other, the exploits of 508th PIR of 101st (US) Airborne Division during Operation Market Garden.*

The initial attack, helped by the bombing and the artillery barrage, went well, but the conditions made the going difficult, particularly for the 3rd Can Inf Div – nicknamed the 'Water Rats' for their work on the Scheldt – who had to contend with flooding along the Waal. Finally, when the German high command accepted that the thrust into the Reichswald was the main attack, reinforcements began to be channelled in and – the Americans still sidelined by the flooding of the Roer dams – the troops that would have been engaged by Operation Grenade were also sucked into the mincing machine, starting with 7. Fallschirmjäger-Division, probably the Germans' best reserve unit. Inexorably, as in Normandy, the British and Canadian attacks pulled more German divisions towards them: 6. Fallschirmjäger, 15. Panzergrenadier, and 116. Panzer. And the floods got deeper. Montgomery gave Crerar reinforcing divisions too: British 43rd (Wessex) and 52nd (Lowland) Inf, and 11th Armoured. The extra men saw the Reichswald and Cleve finally taken.

Above Left: *Booty, as always, was taken – here British soldiers with captured German flags, Kranenburg, 9 February.*

Centre Left: *With the first stage of the operation over, there was now space for the advance to be taken up on a two-corps front. Simonds, therefore, took over the northern units and advanced towards Calcar and Goch (see map p132). The fighting was as bitter as anything the Canadians had had to contend with. Here, trench warfare in the Reichswald.*

Below Left: *This Jagdpanther was put out of action by a 17pdr gun of the 6th Anti-Tank Regiment, RCA, in the Reichswald.*

Opposite:
Above Left: *The third phase of Operation Veritable was across the Hochwald to Xanten – Operation Blockbuster. Fortunately, this coincided with the advance of Ninth (US) Army across the River Roer as Operation Grenade finally got underway. The German defences were insufficient to hold back the rampant Yanks who quickly made up for lost time. Unfortunately, the effects of this advance didn't help First Canadian Army in the Hochwald. They had to fight ghastly battle after ghastly battle as the Fallschirmjäger fought bitterly for every step of ground. Here a trooper of the South Alberta Regiment examines a PzKpfw IV knocked out near Xanten.*

Above Right: *The 7.5cm Pak 40 anti-tank gun position in the Hochwald captured by the action during which Maj F.A. Tilston of the Essex Scottish Regt won the Victoria Cross. It was the second Canadian VC of the operation, Sgt Aubrey Cosens of the Queen's Own Rifles winning his for valour near Udem on 25–26 February.*

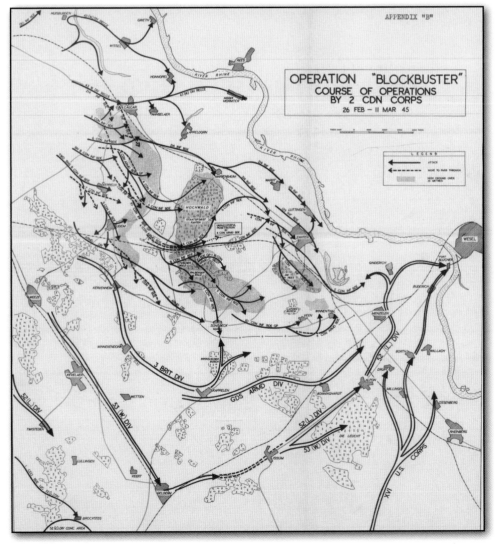

APPENDIX "B"

OPERATION "BLOCKBUSTER"
COURSE OF OPERATIONS
BY 2 CDN CORPS
26 FEB – 11 MAR 45

Below: *And finally it was over. The German forces that could, escaped over the Rhine leaving the Allied armies in charge of the west bank along with 90,000 prisoners and weapons – such as these Panzerfausts.*

British XXX Corps (Lt Gen B.G. Horrocks) was attached to First Canadian Army for Operation Veritable and brought with it Guards Armoured Division (in corps reserve) and other armoured units including 8th Armd Bde, which had just taken part in Operation Blackcock in the Peel Marshes. This M4A1 – a Grizzly, meaning it was built in Canada – has the markings of the British 8th Armd Bde's Sherwood Rangers Yeomanry (the fox's head is the marking for 8th Armd; 996 is that of the Rangers) and can be found at the Bevrijdingsmuseum in Groesbeek. Postwar it served in Portugal and came via the Bovington Tank Museum.

OPERATION PLUNDER: MONTY'S SET-PIECE CROSSING OF THE RHINE

After the heavy fighting during Operations Veritable and Blockbuster, First Canadian Army's involvement in Operation Plunder was limited initially to a brigade – the 9th. First, the Highland Light Infantry of Canada crossed in Buffaloes west of Rees on 24 March under the command of XXX British Corps. Soon rest of the brigade – the Stormont, Dundas and Glengarry Highlanders and the North Nova Scotia Highlanders – joined them. First task was to take Speldrop, defended by Fallschirmjäger; this accomplished, the brigade pushed on towards Emmerich, but were held up at Bienen and Millingen by the German paratroops. By the time Emmerich fell at the end of March, the Canadian bridgehead had been expanded to need the whole of 3rd Can Inf Div, under command of II Canadian Corps, with support from 4th Can Armd Div's tanks firing from across the river.

It was obvious now, with the back of the resistance broken, that the end of the war was in sight. Chewed up on the west of the Rhine, the German forces that were left put up a brave – at times fanatical – resistance but were overpowered from every direction. First Canadian Army had been brought up to strength by Operation Goldflake with I Canadian Corps joining from Italy. The army, therefore, lost I British Corps, after eight months serving with the Canadians.

Right: *As soon as possible bridges were thrown over the Rhine. This wartime (but taken after the battle) aerial photograph of Rees from the south shows Westminster (**A**) and London (**B**) bridges. This photo was taken by W/Op Sgt William H. Oates from an RAF No 295 Squadron Stirling.*

Below Right: *Winston Churchill (**A**) overlooking the Rhine on 4 March, accompanied by Gen H.D.G. Crerar (**B**), Lt Gen G.G. Simonds (**C**), FM Sir Alan Brooke (**D**) and FM Sir Bernard Montgomery (**E**).*

Maj P.R. Griffin, OC A Coy, 1st Can Para Bn at Bergerfurth Wald, Germany, 24 March 1945.

Far Right: *Cpl Fred Topham, VC.*

Below: *Men of the battalion link up with 8th Royal Scots at Bergerfurth on 25 March. Note the 15th Highland Div insignia on the front of the Daimler Dingo scout car.*

Bottom: *Loading a Universal carrier into a Hamilcar for delivery to Germany, 18 March.*

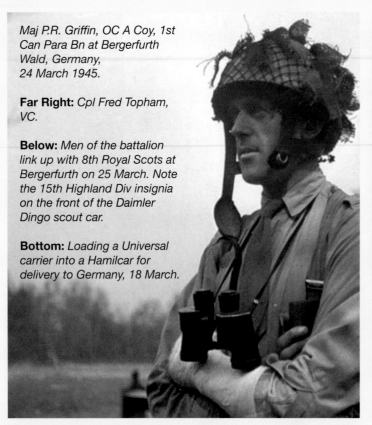

1ST CANADIAN PARACHUTE BATTALION

Operation Varsity was the airborne element of FM Montgomery's last set-piece battle of the war as 21st Army Group – including Ninth (US) Army – made the most northerly crossing of the Rhine. Two airborne divisions dropped: 17th (US) Airborne and 6th (BR) Airborne. Learning from earlier mistakes, the airborne troops were dropped in one airlift and after their own land forces had started crossing the Rhine in order to minimise the risks to the lightly armed airborne troops. The largest single-day airborne drop in history saw high air force casualties – Flak accounted for over 50 aircraft and damaged many more – but the paras achieved their objectives and shattered local opposition. 1st Can Para Bn jumped as part of 3rd (BR) Para Bde. Within minutes of landing it had lost its CO, Lt Col Jeff Nicklin, and command was taken over by Lt Col Fraser Eadie: he was awarded the DSO for his leadership of the battalion from the banks of the Rhine to its final position at Wismar on the Baltic. During the fighting medical orderly Cpl Fred Topham distinguished himself in tending to the wounded and rescuing injured men from a burning carrier. He was awarded the VC in August 1945.

After fighting off the Fallschirmjäger the battalion advanced 285 miles in the next month, reaching Wismar on 2 May 1945 just before the Russians, who were making a determined effort to reach the Danish coast. Hostilities over, the battalion returned to Canada by ship, leaving Europe on 31 May.

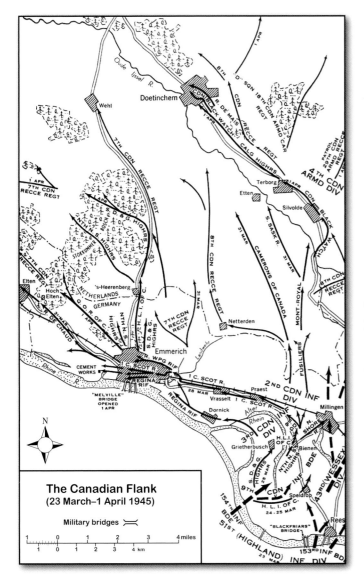

Above: *The Canadian advance from the Rhine.*

Above Right: *Men of the Canadian Grenadier Guards stacking 75mm shells. In the background the regiment's Shermans are ready to support Canadian infantry across the Rhine, 28 March.*

Centre Right: *On 1 April the Highland Light Infantry of Canada liberated 's Heerenberg. There's a memorial, presented in 2010, in the form of an Ordnance QF 25pdr with the markings of 11 Bty, 12th Field Regt, RCA. It serves as a reminder of the 29,000 Canadian gunners who manned 1,100 guns in 38 artillery regiments. 900 died between D-Day and VE-Day.*

Right: *The 9th Can Inf Bde broke the Fallschirmjäger in tense battles around Bienen. The memorial plaques in the churchyard remember a hard battle, in particular by the North Nova Scotia Highlanders, 40 of whom died in the fighting. This plaque, put up in 2000, includes the lines 'Wenn die Sonne glühend versinkt und am Morgen das Licht erwacht, werden wir ihrer gedenken.' ('At the going down of the sun and in the morning we will remember them.')*

Right: *RCE sappers prepare to cross Blackfriars Bridge. Constructed by II Canadian Corps Troops, RCE, this Class 40 low-level Bailey pontoon bridge was one of a number built by the Canadians. This one was at Rees; Melville Bridge at Emmerich was finished on 1 April.*

Centre Right: *Staghound armoured cars of A Squadron, 12th Manitoba Dragoons – the 18th Armoured Car Regt and II Canadian Corps' recce unit. After the war the Dragoons' Staghounds went to the Royal Dutch Army. Note the unit insignia, 44 in a green and blue square with a white band on top denoting corps troops. The corps insignia (see below) is obscured. Having been used as infantry when they landed in Normandy, the advance from the Seine saw the Dragoons first into Bruges (see pp106– 107). The later Mk III version of the Staghound was upgunned with a 75mm-armed Crusader tank turret – this has the older 37mm.*

Below Right: *Bren at the ready, men of 7 Platoon, C Coy, 1st Can Para Bn, dig in at Bergerfurth, west of Hamminkeln, 24 March.*

Below: *Corps vehicle insignia – I (Below) and II (Bottom).*

ROYAL CANADIAN CORPS OF SIGNALS (RCCS)

Every army requires service corps and First Canadian Army was no exception – the Royal Canadian Army Service Corps, the Royal Canadian Electrical and Mechanical Engineers, Royal Canadian Army Medical Corps, Royal Canadian Ordnance Corps and, possibly the most important, the RCCS. Increasingly important for command and control, for artillery and air support, the RCCS provided wireless and line communication for the First Canadian Army. RCCS manned the army and corps signals equipment and each division had its signals units (companies for infantry;

squadrons for armour) usually 728 strong (28 officers and 700 ORs). Within smaller units there were regimental signallers – the trade badge was crossed signal flags on the lower sleeve. By June 1944 the RCCS deployed over 10,000 men in Europe. Signalling still involved much use of telephones and line, as the radios of World War II were not always the most efficient. There was steady improvement, however, and Canada was a leader in both radar and radio manufacturing, improving on a number of the British designs (such as the 19 and 58 wireless sets).

Above: *The main wireless set used by armoured units was the No 19 (example here). It had channels for communications with the regimental net, troop net and internal crew communications. Some tanks also had telephones for infantry contact. Higher up the command chain, armoured units used No 22 sets.*

Above Right: *Infantrymen of D Coy, Régiment de Maisonneuve with a No 18 wireless set, Cuyk, Netherlands, 23 January 1945. This was the standard portable signals set used for communications between companies in the field and battalion HQs. A smaller and lighter set, the No 38, had a short range and was used within the company. Note crossed flags trades badge at right.*

Right: *First Canadian Army Signals, at Zeddam, Netherlands, 4 April 1945. In the background, a Wireless Set No 9 Receiver. The Canadian version of the British No 9 was a big improvement. Canadian companies built many versions of British radio sets, the No 9 developing into the No 52 of 1944. Note RCCS shoulder insignia.*

UNIFORMS AND EQUIPMENT *(by Ed Hallett)*

1 This group of Canadian infantry march through a small village. The weather is clearly warm as several have rolled back the sleeves of their battledress blouses. These veterans have modified the webbing they wear to better suit the demands of life in the field. The water bottles of most men have been moved to sit over their buttocks rather than the hip. The men wear a mixture of Mk II and Mk III helmets, perhaps indicating that some are replacements who were equipped at different times to the rest of the unit. The soldier second from left carries a 2-inch mortar tucked under his right arm.

2 In this summer view, a Canadian tank crew prepares a meal next to their vehicle. The man on the right wears the one-piece tank crew denim overall, produced in a mid-green shade of cotton. The man second from left wears a sleeveless woollen pullover that may be either the issue item, or a 'comforts' piece knitted for him by one of the army of civilian knitters who produced clothing to supplement official channels. The black beret worn by some of the crew was adopted as a standard piece of headwear for armoured

crews across both the British and Canadian armies. It was very practical as the black prevented oil stains from showing and its soft nature allowed it to be worn under a radio headset.

3 This group illustrates some of the variety of uniform and accoutrements that could be seen in the field. Two of the men carry their revolvers in Canadian-produced holsters which were larger and more curved in shape than British examples. Two of the crew have been issued with tan-coloured tank crew overalls, known colloquially as a 'pixie' or 'zoot' suit. This was a one-piece, lined garment that was worn over battledress to keep the wearer warm in the frigid metal interior of an AFV. Some of the men have also been issued with the Canadian-produced high leather boots with integral buckled cuff that was issued in limited numbers.

4 These men of the Lincoln and Welland Regt have been issued with sets of loose white cotton camouflage smocks and trousers to go over their standard battledress. This was effective camouflage against the snows of western Europe in the winter of 1944/45. The smock had a hood that could be pulled up to offer some

wind protection to the sides of the head as seen by three of the men. The helmets are also covered in a white camouflage cover. The armies of the Empire were better equipped than their US counterparts who were forced to borrow white uniforms or improvise them from bed sheets. The men wear inflatable life preservers as they have just finished an operation on the Kapelsche Veer in canoes (see p131).

5 Boarding a Buffalo APC, these men show use of equipment from late in the war. Most men have picks or shovels attached to their webbing to allow them to more rapidly dig a shell scrape, most men having ditched the issued two-part entrenching tool as inadequate. The man at **A** carries a Bren gun. He has acquired a second water bottle cradle he's using to carry his mess tins, freeing up space in his pack and making it easier to access them when it is time for food, this being a common practice amongst Canadian soldiers. Some of the men seem to be wearing rubber Canadian snow boots which were heavy-duty moulded rubber boots secured with laces and a pair of spring clips at the top.

6 This Canadian soldier, escorting German prisoners, is well wrapped up against the cold. Over his battledress he wears a camouflaged Denison smock, with scarf and knitted woollen gloves. Over this is worn the ubiquitous 37-pattern webbing. Canada had two main manufacturers of webbing accoutrements: Zephyr Loom and Textile Ltd of Ontario and Montreal Suspender and Umbrellas Ltd.

7 Deep in the Reichswald forest in March 1945, the central soldier clearly illustrates the 18 Set radio, which is worn on his back. All the soldiers in this view wear the earlier Mk II helmet, still in widespread use right up until the end of the war. The man in the centre has covered his helmet with a camouflage net and tucked a shell dressing underneath, ensuring he has one rapidly to hand should the worst happen. He and the radioman wear lightweight rubberised gas capes as a waterproof outer layer, the bulge designed to go over a pack is clearly visible on the soldier to the left. Officially this practice was frowned upon as it wore out the capes much faster than if they were left rolled up, but it was a practical solution to inadequate wet weather clothing.

6 The Last Rites

Op 17 april 1945 staken
de geallieerde strijdkrachten
de IJssel over en werd
de stad Kampen bevrijd.

17 april 1995

It still seems surprising that the Germans fought on into March and April. They trusted Hitler and his talk of secret weapons, perhaps.The strong chance of being shot for desertion was a definite risk – 700 men a month were sentenced to death for *Fahnenflucht* (lit: flight from the colours = desertion) during the second half of 1944. For whatever reason, they did keep fighting and right up to the bitter end there was no let up. Often this just meant snipers and landmines; sometimes, however, it involved small

Left: *Memorial at Kampen on the IJssel River, crossed on 17 April 1945. The insignia is that of the 17th Duke of York's Canadian Hussars, the 7th Recce Regt of 3rd Can Inf Div.*

Right: *Memorial to long-time Canadian cohorts, the Polar Bears – British 49th (West Riding) Inf Div – at Rosendaal in Belgium.*

Below: *Operation Destroyer saw the Polar Bears, along with 11th Can Inf Bde clear the Island (Betuwe), fought over since Operation Market Garden.*

battles every bit as hard as in previous months but without the duration.

For First Canadian Army, the last two months of the war saw the largest all-Canadian force of the war fighting together. With I British Corps replaced by I Canadian Corps from Italy, the army still benefited from the cosmopolitan inclusion of the 1st Polish Armd Div and the Polar Bears – the British 49th (West Riding) Inf Div. However, for all the size of the army, I Canadian Corps was not as large as the forces opposing them, Heeresgruppe H under Genoberst Johannes Blaskowitz – over 120,000 of varying quality.

Blaskowitz had more to worry about than the Canadians. The Hunger Winter of 1944–45 had reached such a pitch that five days after 49th Division attacked Arnhem on 12 April, both sides agreed to halt aggressive action on the Grebbe Line. The Germans agreed not to proceed with the demolitions and inundations. Some 20,000 civilians died of the privations, but had it not been for the ceasefire and relief operations, it could have been a lot worse.

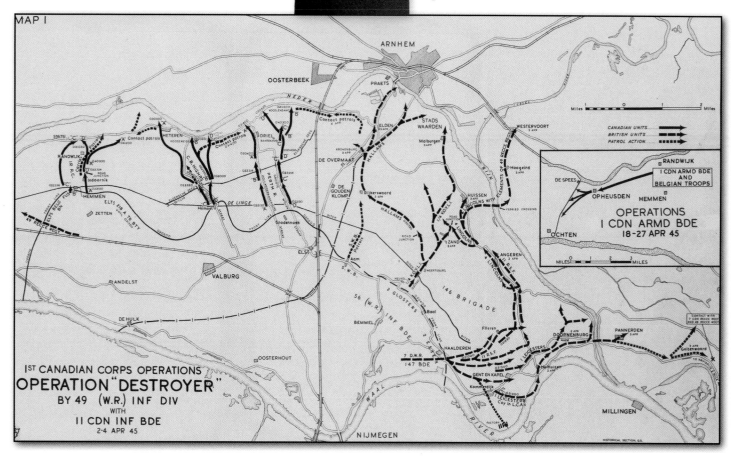

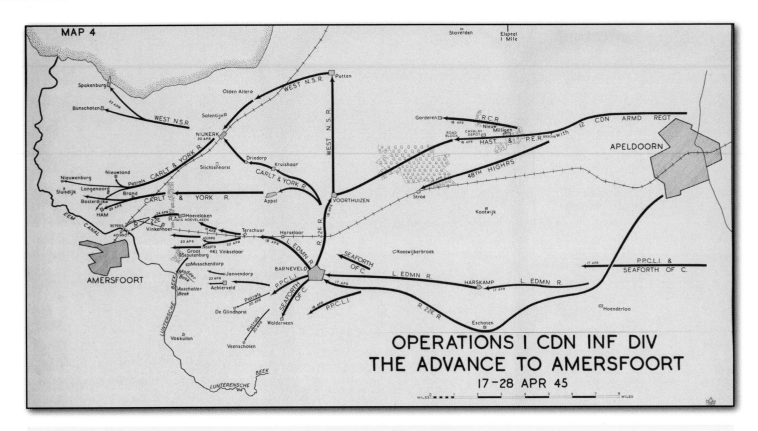

I CANADIAN CORPS

The end of February saw the move of the Canadian forces in Italy to north-west Europe. I Corps' GOC since November 1944 was Lt Gen Charles Foulkes. Operational from 15 March 1945, 5th Can Armd Div came under command in February and 1st Can Inf Div on 13 April – it had arrived in March but came initially under II Canadian Corps. Also fighting with I Canadian Corps was British 49th (West Riding) Inf Div – the 'Polar Bears'.

I Corps main units are listed below.

Corps Troops
1st Armoured Car Regt (Royal Canadian Dragoons)
7th Anti-Tank Regt, RCA
1st LAA Regt, RCA

1st Armoured Division (Brig W. C. Murphy from 27 February)
3rd Armd Recce Regt (Governor General's Horse Guards)

1st Armd Bde
11th Armd Regt (Ontario Regt)
12th Armd Regt (Three Rivers Regt)
14th Armd Regt (Calgary Regt)

1st Infantry Division (Maj Gen Harry Foster)
4th Armd Recce Regt (4th Princess Louise Dragoon Guards)

1st Inf Bde
Royal Canadian Regt
Hastings and Prince Edward Regt
48th Highlanders of Canada

2nd Inf Bde
Princess Patricia's Canadian Light Infantry
Seaforth Highlanders of Canada
Loyal Edmonton Regt

3rd Inf Bde
Royal 22e Regt
Carleton and York Regt
West Nova Scotia Regt

5th Armoured Division (Maj Gen B.M. Hoffmeister)
5th Armd Bde
2nd Armd Regt (Lord Strathcona's Horse (Royal Canadians))
5th Armd Regt (8th Princess Louise's (New Brunswick) Hussars)
9th Armd Regt (British Columbia Dragoons)
Westminster Regt (motorised)

11th Inf Bde
11th Independent MG Company (Princess Louise Fusiliers)
1st Bn, Perth Regt
1st Bn, Cape Breton Highlanders
1st Bn, Irish Regt of Canada
11th Inf Bde Ground Defence Pl (Lorne Scots)

+ RCA, RCE, RCASC, RCOC, RCCS, RCAMC, RCEME, RMP etc

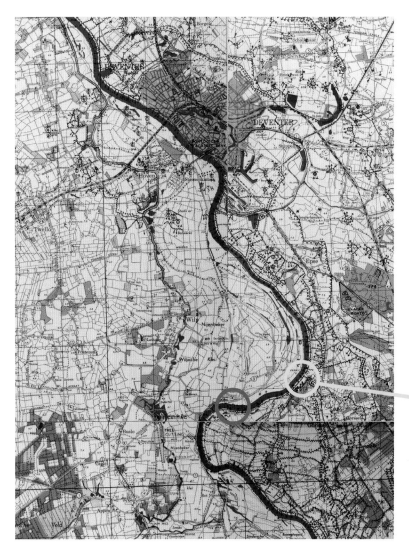

Above and Opposite: *I Canadian Corps approached the job of clearing the Western Netherlands methodically, the first step being to clear the Betuwe, that fought-over low-lying ground between Nijmegen and Arnhem that had been a source of irritation to both sides since Operation Market Garden in September 1944. The Polar Bears, 11th Can Inf Bde and 1st Can Armd Bde accomplished this with Operation Destroyer (see map p 145). Next, rather than attack Arnhem head on, the 1st Can Inf Div thrust across the IJssel between Zutphen (cleared by 3rd Can Inf Div on 7/8 April on its way north) and Deventer (Above). The 2nd Can Inf Bde – the PPCLI and the Seaforths – crossed at Gorssel in Operation Cannonshot, starting on 11 April. Having crossed and beaten off a counterattack, a bridge was built and 1st and 3rd Can Inf Bdes headed for Apeldoorn. Further south Arnhem fell rapidly and the 49th Div attacked through Ede as the 5th Can Armd Div headed towards the IJsselmeer.*

Above and Top Right: *The memorial at Gorssel near where the PPCLI crossed the IJssel (yellow circle shows where the bridge went up; red circle shows where the Seaforths crossed).*

Centre Right: *The bridge at Gorssel.*

Right: *Soldiers of the PPCLI and Buffalo amphibious vehicles used to cross the IJssel River on 11 April.*

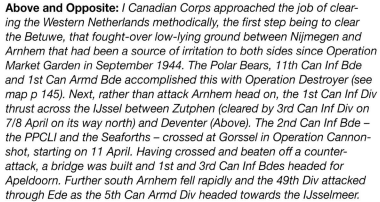

Above: *This Sherman 105mm can be found in Ede. It is in the markings of the Calgary Regt which worked with the British 49th (West Riding) Inf Div to liberate the town, lying to the west of Arnhem, on 17 April. As we look at it, on the right is the 1st Can Armd Bde insignia (black and red stripes with Maple Leaf); at left, the markings of the Calgary Regt (175 in a blue and brown square).*

Above Right: *Private K.O. Earl of the Perth Regiment resting in the woods north of Arnhem, 15 April.*

Below: *Arnhem fell after street fighting in April 1945. The Polar Bears assaulted over the canal in a major operation involving softening up by Spitfires and Typhoons, a massive artillery barrage and a diversion by the so-called Murphyforce to the south of the city. The first wave was the 2nd Glosters who were followed by 2nd South Wales Borderers. Only 12 hours later a Bailey bridge was in place and soon after that a pontoon ferry for the tanks of the Ontario Regt. By the 16th it was all over and the 5th Can Armd Div headed north while the 49th headed west.*

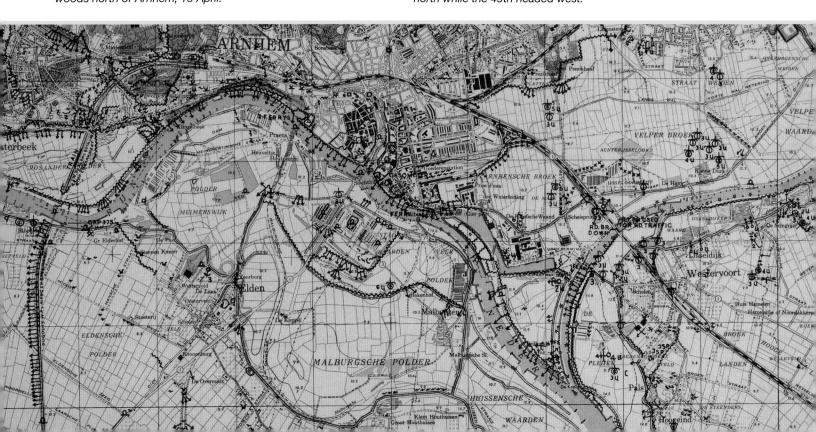

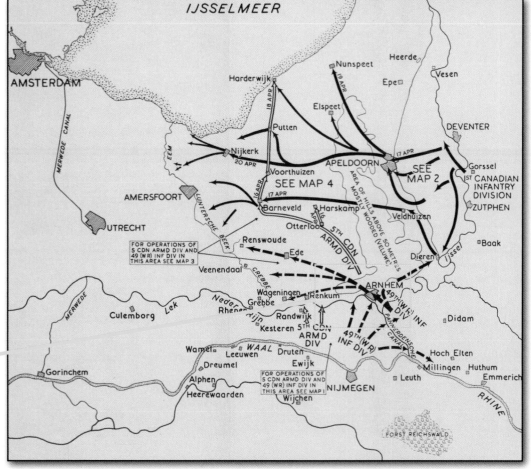

Above: *Shortly after the second battle of Arnhem the tanks of the 5th Can Armd Div headed north in Operation Cleanser. They reached the IJsselmeer – what used to be known as the Zuider Zee – on the 18th. Here, civilians are out to greet them at Harderwijk on 19 April. On the way north, at Otterlo on the night of 16/17 April, they were attacked by Germans desperate to join their forces in the west. In an intense battle, the Germans suffered 300 casualties.*

Left: *The Canadian advance west was halted at the Grebbe Line. With bombing missions over, Allied air forces dropped food to the starving civilian population – the RAF, RCAF, RAAF and Polish AF in Operation Manna 29 April–7 May, and the USAAF in Operation Chowhound, 1–8 May. From 2 May these were followed up by the ground-based Operation Faust.*

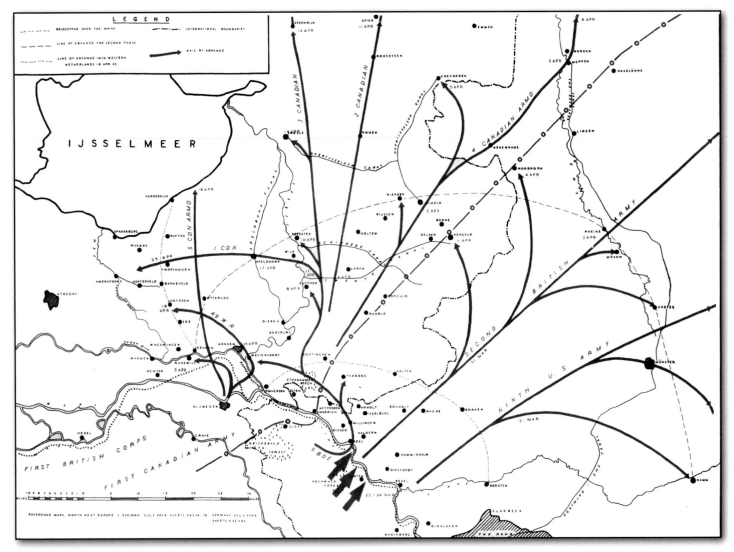

Above: *II Canadian Corps operations in April 1945 saw 4th Can Armd Div advance alongside Second British Army towards Wilhelmshaven and Bremen. They were flanked by 1st Polish from mid-April. The 2nd and 3rd Inf Divs headed north after Operation Plunder, the 2nd to Groningen and 3rd to Leeuwarden. Once these had been liberated, 2nd moved northeast to Oldenburg to support the British attack on Bremen and the 3rd attacked Leer in Operation Duck, crossing the River Ems towards Emden. 5th Can Armd headed for the IJsselmeer and reached it on 18 April and then moved north at the beginning of May. It attacked and took Delfzijl in an operation that involved Dutch troops.*

Left: *Groningen – and 5,000 German troops – surrendered on 16 April but not before street-fighting and casualties to the Canadians (209 with 43 dead) and civilians (110).*

Opposite, Centre Left: *Tactical HQ of Les Fusiliers Mont-Royal, Munderloh, Germany, 29 April.*

Opposite, Below Left: *Dutch children watching Canadian artillery cross a temporary bridge, Balkbrug, 11 April.*

151

Left: *Poor Doetinchem was badly bombed and its centre gutted on 21 and 23 March. This tank is a memorial to the Fort Garry Horse which liberated the town on 2 April.*

Below: *Infantrymen of the South Saskatchewan Regiment during mopping-up operations along the Oranje Canal, 12 April.*

Bottom: *Infantrymen of the Royal Hamilton Light Infantry aboard a Sherman tank of B Sqn, Fort Garry Horse, en route to Groningen, Netherlands, 13 April.*

The main II Canadian Corps thrust after Operation Plunder was north and northeast as it advanced alongside Second British Army towards the Bremen. There were hard battles, particularly around Groningen, Oldenburg, Leer and Delfzijl but, after 3rd Inf Div crossed the Ems and closed in on Emden, the Germans' unconditional surrender took place.

On the 4th the army was still fighting. On the 5th it was all over – 333 days after landing on the Normandy beaches. Gen Simonds in Bad Zwischenahn accepted the surrender of Gen Straube, while in Wageningen Gen Foulkes, GOC I Corps, provided Generaloberst Blaskowitz with his copy of the surrender document. On 7 May, at Rheims, the formal surrender was signed.

This Page: *Today, in Zutphen it's the Canadians' Bridge at the bottom of Deventerweg. Then, it was an obstacle – a downed bridge over the River Berkel – for C Coy, North Shore Regt to negotiate on 7 April. Here stretcher bearers are helped across.*

Below Right: *Infantrymen of the North Shore Regt lifting mines on the approach to the bridge.*

Below: *Looking back towards Deventer, a safe lane has been marked out with tape.*

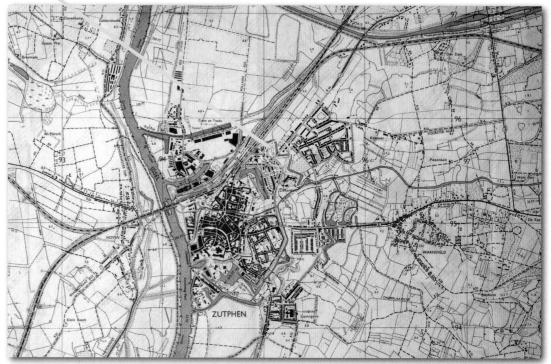

Above: *Entry of the 4th Can Armd Div into Delden on 4 April. The vehicle is an M7 Priest SP gun converted into a Kangaroo armoured command post. There's a Ram Kangaroo behind it.*

Above Right: *A Canadian Grenadier Guards' Firefly in Almelo on 5 April. 4th Armd Div's armoured brigade included the 21st, 22nd (the Grenadier Guards) and 28th Armd Regts.*

Below: *Infantryman of A Coy, Highland Light Infantry of Canada, heading towards boats on the Ems River to attack Leer, Germany, 28 April. In his left hand is a three-round mortar carry pack and he's wearing an inflatable life protector.*

Below: *The position of First Canadian Army at the end of hostilities.*

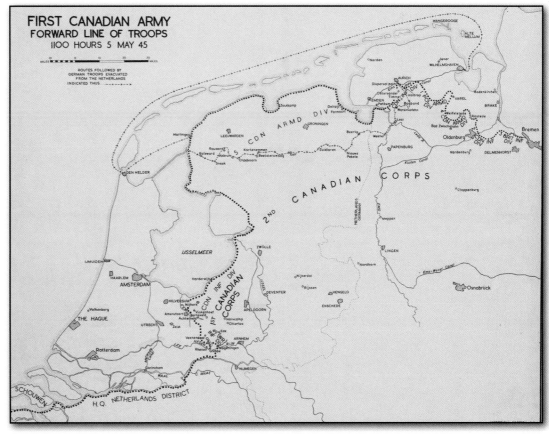

Below: *The National Netherlands Liberation monument remembers the part played by the Canadians. 'Man with Two Hats' in Apeldoorn since 2000 was made by Henk Visch. An identical figure can be found in Ottawa's Commissioners Park.*

Right: *Surrender! Lt Gen Charles Foulkes (left centre), GOC I Canadian Corps, issues instructions to Generaloberst Johannes Blaskowitz, in the auditorium of the University of Wageningen, 5 May 1945.*

Opposite, Centre: *A USAAF B-17 drops supplies over the western Netherlands during Operation Chowhound, 1–8 May.*

Opposite, Below: *German soldiers entering a concentration area to be disarmed by men of I Canadian Corps, Amsterdam, 9 May – note the Polar Bears' insignia.*

Above Left: *East meets west – 1st Can Para Bn spoldier shaking hands with a Russian soldier, Wismar, Germany, 4 May.*

Above Right: *Lt G. Murray Williams of HQ Coy, 1st Can Para Bn, on a Norton motorcycle during the advance to Wismar. Some rode on the back of tanks, others used whatever they could find to get to the Baltic before the Russians could push round to the Danish border.*

Right: *1st Polish Armd Div advanced on 4th Can Armd Div's left, crossing the Ems and ending in Wilhelmshaven where Gen Maczek accepted the surrender of forces in the area.*

7 Remembrance

The Commonwealth War Graves Commission was established as the Imperial War Graves Commission by royal charter in 1917. Its mission, identified on its excellent website, 'honours the 1.7 million men and women who died in the armed forces of the British Empire during the First and Second World Wars, and ensures they will never be forgotten.' There are more than 23,000 locations in 150 countries, and in each there is equality of treatment for the dead irrespective of rank or religion.

Brainchild of Sir Fabian Ware whose Red Cross unit had begun recording and caring for the graves they could find on the battlefields of World War I, the design of the cemeteries and memorials was chosen from the ideas of three important architects of the period: Sir Herbert Baker, Sir Reginald Blomfield and Sir Edwin Lutyens.

The CWGC commemorates more than 45,000 people who died while serving with the Canadian and Newfoundland forces. Of First Canadian Army's dead, a number were taken home for burial. Many remained in European cemeteries including specifically Canadian cemeteries such as those at Bretteville-sur-Laize on the road between Caen and Falaise (**Opposite**); Bény-sur-Mer – a stone's throw from Juno Beach (**Above Right**); and Bergen-op-Zoom near the Beveland causeway where many of those who died cleariung the Scheldt are buried (**Centre Right**). There are also many Canadians remembered in Commonwealth cemeteries such as that at the Reichswald Forest War Cemetery (**Below Right**) near Kleve.

The cemeteries are immaculate, wonderfully tended and cared for, colouful with flowers and shrubs, and much visited at all times of year.

CREDITS & BIBLIOGRAPHY

CREDITS

Thanks are due to Elly for design work, Richard Wood and the military cyclists for the over-the-ground research, Richard Drew of www.Atlantikwall.co.uk, Battlefieldhistorian. com for generous provision of photographs, Battle Detective Tom Timmermans, Simon Kooter and Richard Charlton Taylor for reading the manuscript and making helpful comments, Alison Wilson from the Balmer Hotel, and, of course, Leo Marriott.

The many maps come from a variety of sources: pp28 and pp102–103 from the online resources of the University of Texas, Perry-Castañeda Library Map Collection; p8 info from Stacey (1970); p13 Stacey (1955); p19 (both)info fromFeasby (1956); pp64, 72, 93, 139 Stacey (1960).The others are from the Reports by Historical Section Canadian Military HQ: pp74, 76 No 131; pp81, 85, 88 No 169; p94 No 139; pp99, 101, 106, 108 No 183; pp111 (both), 114 No 188; pp129, 131 No 173; p132 No 155; p135 No 171; pp145, 146, 149 No 39; p150 No 152; p153 No 56. The Canadian maps are © All rights reserved reproduced with the permission of DND/CAF 2014. Otherwise the artwork is, as usual, by Mark Franklin. Info for map on p84 is from Bechthold (2005) and Jarymowyzcz (1998).

Battlefield Historian: *1, 4–5, 7, 13B, 18, 27, 34, 38 (all), 39 IT, 40T, 41B, 42T, 42BR, 43T, 46B, 47T and B, 48T, 50C and B, 59T, 63C, 64T, 65B, 66TL, 67T, 69T, 70TR, 70 BR, 71TR, 71BR, 73T, 73BR, 74B, 75TL, 75BR, 79BL, 80 (all), 82BR, 84B, 85TR, 85BR, 87B, 89TR, 89BL, 94BL, 95T, 140C, 143/7, 148TL;* **Colin Baxter:** *24T;* **Belham Lawn Hotel:** *22B (all);* **Richard Drew:** *49BR, 104BL, 104BR;* **Library and Archives of Canada:** *9T 137186, 9C 174501, 9B 174496, 11T PA-114820, 11B PA-37483, 12T e999902081-u, 14T PA-137184, 14C PA-142659, 14B 4232647, 15 PA-116851, 16T 4752276, 16B 4752278,19BR e010786478-v8, 20A PA-177094, 20BL PA-213630, 20BL PA-177347, 21TL PA-136281, 21TR PA-167300, 21B PA-179910, 22T PA-188676, 23T PA-137130, 23CR PA-136993, 25T PA-132811, 25B PA-129059, 26T 4950978, 26C PA-069252, 26BL RCN A679, 26BR PA-157805, 30T 3941005, 30BL Lt Ken Bell/LAC PA-132882, 30BR PA-131507, 31T PA-191017, 31BL PA-191020, 31BR PA-191020, 33T PA-191017, 43B 4233767, 45BL, 46T, 54CL PA-133100, 54CR PA-136999, 54BL PA-211637, 54BR PA-204971, 55T PA-182953, 55B, 55C PA-116514, 57TL PA-179151, 57TR PA-179678, 57C e002852749, 57R PA-114599, 60BR PA-191065, 66TR PA-114578, 67BR PA-141890, 68TL PA-190907, 68TR PA-133103, 69C 3724322, 69BL PA-128794, 69BR PA-131431, 70TL PA-140191, 70BL PA-190810, 71TL PA-169269, 71CR PA-204952, 71BL PA-131437, 73BL PA-190147, 75TR PA-162681, 75BL PA-162728, 76BL PA-162667, 76BR PA-136857, 77T PA-129128, 77C PA-131382, 77BL PA-131393, 77BC PA-140189, 77BR PA-153423, 79TR, 79BR, 81 4233175, 82TR PA-074094, 90T 4002571, 90B 4002572, 91T e002344097, 94BR PA-204737, 95C PA-213985, 95BR 4233288, 96BL PA-131233, 97T PA-173420 97BL PA-130906, 97BR, 98BL PA-174462, 98BR PA-136333, 99BL PA-131231, 103C, 103B PA-167981, 107TL&TR, 108B PA-167199, 113BL PA-173534, 113BR, 114B PA-137147, 116T e999909568_s1-u, 115 BR e999909569-u, 118BL PA-113670, 118TR, 119BL 4233653, 119BR PA-133330, 120BL, 120BR PA-179797, 122TR e004665474, 123TL PA-138420, 123BR PA-137145, 125R e999909503-u, 126BR PA-136756, 127T e999909506-u, 128 PA-113696, 131AC PA-142421, 132TL PA-191136, 132BR PA-167115, 133TL PA-140645, 133CL PA-161316, 133BL PA-161317, 134TL PA-191213, 134CL PA-192881, 134BL PA-132454, 135TL PA-114964, 135TR PA-113683, 135BR PA-192081, 137B PA-143952, 138TR PA-162026, 138TR, 138CR PA-137349, 138BR PA-137336, 139TR PA-134433, 140TL PA-177853, 140CL PA-144144, 140BL PA-162031, 141TL PA-190219, 141TR PA-190099, 141BR PA-130918, 142/2 PA-133978, 142/3 PA-131263, 143/4, 143/5 3239986, 146TL, 146BL PA-140693, 146CR, 148TR PA-166368, 148B e999909533-u, 149T 3200390, 150B PA-130923, 151CL PA-146281, 151CR PA-113908, 151BL PA-134486, 151BR PA-130941, 152TR PA-133331, 152C e999909931-u, 152BL, 152BR PA-138283, 153TL PA-131627, 153TR PA-130911, 153BR PA-190924, 154TR PA-138588, 154BR PA-134395, 155TL PA-150930, 155TR PA-206876;* **Narodowe Archiwum Cyfrowe** (Polish Archives): *109TL, 109BR, 117TR, 117BL, 130T&C, 131T, 155B;* NARA: *10, 72, 102BR, 105T, 116BL, 122BR, 124T, 129T, 142/1, 154CR;* **Nationaal Archief,** the Dutch National Archives: *21BL, 123BR, 125BL, 143/6, 146BR;* **PISM:** *87C;* **USAF:** *36T, 37T, 51T and B, 95BL, 106T Dunkirk 2;* **WikiCommons:** *17BL (wallycacsabre/ WikiC), 17TR (Phlyer/WikiC CC BY-SA 3.0), 23CL (Murga-troyd49 CC BY-SA 4.0), 37C (René Hourdry CC BY-SA 4.0), 39B France-335, 51CB (Tristan Nitot, CC BY-SA 3.0), 63TR (Burtonne, CC BY-SA 3.0), 63B (Pahcal123, CC BY-SA 4.0), 67BL (Normandywarguide.com), 96T (My father, CC BY-SA 1.0), 100B (Michel wal, CC BY-SA 3.0), 108T (Friedrich Tellberg), 110 (NASA), 114B (John Scholte), 116BR (Txllxt Tx-llxT, CC BY-SA 4.0), 118TR (Spotter2, CC BY-SA 3.0), 118BR (Mejamieson, CC BY-SA 3.0), 120BR (Edwin Hamelink, CC BY-SA 3.0 nl), 120TR Paul Hermans, 121TL (https://nieuwvliet-online.de/denkmal-hickman-bruecke), 121TR (Marc Ryckaert, CC BY-SA 4.0), 126BL (Baykedevries, CC BY-SA 3.0 nl), 144 (Pa3ems, CC BY-SA 3.0), 145 (L.M.Tangel), 146TR (Pacobobo, CC BY-SA 3.0 nl), 152TL (JeroenJerome, CC BY-SA 4.0), 159 (Jaylimo84, CC BY-SA 4.0);* **Richard Wood:** *12B.*

BIBLIOGRAPHY

Online sources include:
http://ww2today.com http://ww2talk.com
http://www.tracesofwar.com/
https://scholars.wlu.ca/

Books and magazine articles
After the Battle: the quarterly magazine never fails to provide information and enlightenment.

Bechthold, Mike: 'Lost in Normandy The Odyssey of Worthington Force, 9 August 1944'; *Canadian Military History:* Vol 14: Iss 1&2, 2005.

Bernage, Georges: *Gold, Juno, Sword;* Heimdal, 2003.

Buckley, John: *Monty's Men: The British Army and the Liberation of Europe;* Yale University Press, 2013.

Buckley, John: *Victory and Defeat? Perceptions of the British Army in Northwest Europe, 1944–1945; Global War Studies, 2013.*

Copp, Terry: *Fields of Fire;* Uni Toronto Press, 2003.

Copp, Terry: *The Brigade;* Stackpole Books, 2007.

Copp, Terry & Bechthold, Mike: *The Canadian Battlefields in Northwest Europe 1944–1945 A Visitor's Guide; Canadian Military History:* Vol 14: Iss 1&2, 2005.

Didden, Jack: *Fighting Spirit: Kampfgruppe Chill and the German recovery in the West between 4 September and 9 November 1944, A case study.*

Ellis, Maj L.F.: *Victory in the West Vol I The Battle of Normandy;* HMSO, 1962.

Ellis, Maj L.F.: *Victory in the West Vol II The Defeat of Germany;* HMSO, 1968.

Feasby, W.R. (Ed): *Official History of the Canadian Medical Services 1939–1945 Vol 1 Organization and Campaigns;* Minister of National Defense, 1956.

Ford, Ken: *Battle Zone Normandy 3 Juno Beach;* Sutton Publishing, 2004.

Ford, Ken: *Campaign 74 The Rhineland;* Osprey, 2000.

Ford, Ken: *Campaign 178 The Rhine Crossings;* Osprey, 2006.

Ford, Ken: *D-Day Commando;* Sutton Publishing, 2003.

Gullachsen, Arthur: 'Destroying the Panthers: The Effect of Allied Combat Action on I./SS Panzer Regiment 12 in Normandy, 1944'; *Canadian Military History:* Vol. 25: Iss. 2, Article 13, 2016.

Harclerode, Peter: 'Go To It' The Illustrated History of 6th Airborne Division; Caxton Editions, 2000.

Henry, Hugh: 'The Calgary Tanks at Dieppe' *Canadian Military History:* Vol. 4: Iss. 1/6, 1995.

Jarymowycz, Roman Johann: 'Canadian Armour in Normandy: Operation "Totalize" and the Quest for Operational Manoeuvre'; *Canadian Military History,* Vol. 7: Iss. 2, Article 3; 1998.

Milner, Marc: *Stopping the Panzers;* Uni Press Kansas, 2014.

Milner, Marc: 'The Guns of Bretteville: 13th Field Regiment, RCA, and the defence of Bretteville-l'Orgueilleuse, 7–10 June 1944'; *Canadian Military History:*, Vol. 16: Iss. 4, Article 2, 2007.

Moulton, J.L.: *Battle for Antwerp;* Ian Allan Ltd, 1978.

Pallud, Jean Paul: *Rückmarsch! The German Retreat From Normandy Then and Now; After the Battle:* 2007.

Patterson, David: 'Outside the Box: A New Perspective on Operation Windsor—The Rationale Behind the Attack on Carpiquet, 4 July 1944'; *Canadian Military History:* Vol. 17: Iss. 2, Article 7, 2008.

Pellerin, R. Daniel: ' "You Have Shut Up the Jerries" Canadian Counter-Battery Work in the Clearing of the Breskens Pocket, October–November 1944'; *Canadian Military History:* Vol. 21: Iss. 3, Article 3, 2015.

Ramsay, Winston: *D-Day Then and Now;* two volumes After the Battle, 1995.

Ramsay, Winston *The Defeat of Germany Then and Now;* After the Battle, 2015.

Rottmann, Gordon L.: *Elite 209 Victory 1945;* Osprey, 2015.

Silz, John: *River Assault – Operation Duck;* Travelogue 219, 2014.

Stacey, Col C.P.: *Arms, Men and Governments The War policies of Canada 1939–1945;* Minister of National Defense, 1970.

Stacey, Col C.P.: *Official History of the Canadian Army in the Second World War Vol I Six Years of War;* Minister of National Defense, 1955.

Stacey, Col C.P.: *Official History of the Canadian Army in the Second World War Vol III The Victory Campaign;* Minister of National Defense, 1960.

Windsor, Lee A.: 'Too Close for the Guns!' 9 Canadian Infantry Brigade in the Battle for Rhine Bridgehead; *Canadian Military History:* Vol. 12: Iss. 2, Article 2, 2003.

Zaloga, Steven J.: *Campaign 293 Downfall 1945;* Osprey, 2016.

Zuehlke, Mark: *Assault on Juno;* Raven Books, 2012.

Documents retrieved through Ike Skelton Combined Arms Research Library Digital Library
Clearing of the Scheldt, 21st Army Group.
Notes on the Operations of 21 Army Group, 6.6.44–5.5.45.
Report on Operation Veritable.

GLOSSARY & ABBREVIATIONS

1CACR 1st Canadian Armoured Carrier Regt—one of two units (the other was 49th APCR Armoured Personnel Carrier Regt) serving under 79th Armd Div that were used by 21st Army Group

2e DB *2nd Division Blindée* = French 2nd Armd Div

2TAF 2nd Tactical Air Force, RAF

79th Armoured Division Unit that controlled all British specialised armour: Crab anti-mine flails, Crocodile or Wasp flamethrowers, Kangaroo APCs, AVREs, Buffalo LVTs, etc

AFV Armoured fighting vehicle

AGRA Army Group Royal Artillery

ALG advanced landing ground

APC armoured personnel carrier

ATk anti-tank

Army group The largest military units of the Allies and the Germans, they each controlled a number of armies.

(L/H)AA (light/heavy) antiaircraft

Armd armoured

ARV armored recovery vehicle

AVRE armoured vehicle, Royal Engineers – combat engineer vehicle armed with a 290mm spigot mortar

Bde brigade

BEF British Expeditionary Force (sent to France in 1940)

Bn battalion (usually infantry)

CAFA Canadian Armed Forces Abroad

Coy company

Can Canadian

Cdo Commando, used of the soldier and the units. RAF Cdos protected airfields; RN Cdos beachheads. The Army and RM Cdos were used mainly to spearhead landing operations and were used as such at D-Day and the Rhine crossings

CIGS Chief of the Imperial General Staff (Brit), for most of the war Field Marshal Alan Brooke

CRCA Commander, RCA

CWGC Commonwealth War Graves Commission

DD Duplex Drive—tanks, usually Shermans, modified to allow flotation and powered river crossing

Doppelschartenstand Gun casemate that allowed the weapon to pivot and fire in two diections

DUKW amphibious load carrier

Festung fortress

FG fighter group

FJR *Fallschirmjäger Regiment* = German paratrooper. II./FJR6 = second battalion of 6th FJ Regt

FOO forward observation officer

Formstein concrete blocks used to construct some bunkers

FS fighter squadron

GFM *Generalfeldmarschall* = German field marshal

GenLt *Generalleutnant* = German lieutenant general

GSGS Geographical Section General Staff produced maps for the British armed forces

Heeresgruppe German army group

KG *Kampfgruppe* = German battle group, a combinations of troops that happened to be available at a given time. Usually named for their commander

KO knocked out. If used about armored vehicles this didn't necessarily mean that they were destroyed. Battlefield recovery, refurbishment in battlefield workshops, and reuse in battle was frequent on both sides

KOSB King's Own Scottish Borderers (British regiment)

Kwk *Kampfwagenkanone* = German tank gun

LC Landing craft types: **A** assault; **G** gun; **I** infantry; **L** large; **R** rocket; **VP** vehicle/personnel. RN contingents brought craft across Europe for use in the major river crossings

LRC light recce car

LS landing ship types: **I** infantry; **T** tank

LVT landing vehicle tracked aka Alligator or Buffalo

(L/M/H)MG (light/medium/heavy) machine gun

MAA *Marine-Artillerie-Abteilung* = German naval artillery unit

MKB *Marine-Küsten-Batterie* = German coastal gun battery

mor mortar

MTB motor torpedo boat

NCO non-commissioned officer (sergeant, corporal)

OB West/Süd etc *Oberbefehlshaber West/Süd* = German C-in-C West/South

Genoberst *Generaloberst* = German general

(G)OC (general) officer commanding

OR other rank (Brit)

Pak *Panzerabwehrkanone* = German anti-tank gun

PIAT Projector Infantry Anti-tank

PPCLI Princess Patricia's Canadian Light Infantry

PzGr *Panzergrenadier* = German armored infantry

PzKpfw *Panzerkampfwagen* = German tank

PzT *Panzerturm* = German armoured turret

RAAF Royal Australian Air Force

Ranks: Officers – Field Marshal (FM), Lieutenant General (Lt Gen), Major General (Maj Gen), General (Gen), Brigadier (Brig), Colonel (Col), Lieutenant Colonel (Lt Col), Major (Maj), Captain (Capt), Lieutenant (Lt), Second Lieutenant (2Lt), Regimental/Company Sergeant Major (RSM/CSM), Corporal (Cpl), Lance Corporal (LCpl), Trooper (Tpr)/Private (Pte)/Sapper (Spr)

R(C)A Royal (Canadian) Artillery

R(C)AC Royal (Canadian) Armoured Corps

R(C)AF Royal (Canadian) Air Force

R(C)AMC Royal (Canadian) Army Medical Corps

R(C)ASC Royal (Canadian) Army Service Corps

R(C)CS Royal (Canadian) Chaplain Service

R(C)CS Royal (Canadian) Corps of Signals

R(C)E Royal (Canadian) Engineers

R(C)EME Royal (Canadian) Electrical and Mechanical Engineers

R(C)N Royal (Canadian) Navy

R(C)OC Royal (Canadian) Ordnance Corps

RCR Royal Canadian Regiment

recce reconnaissance

RHLI Royal Hamilton Light Infantry – the Rileys

Ringstand gun position with a pivot to allow gun all-round traverse

RRC Royal Rifles of Canada Regt

(C/R)SM (Company/Regimental) Sergeant Major

RTR Royal Tank Regiment

RWR Royal Winnipeg Rifles

SBG small box girder bridge

Sqn squadron (usually armoured or aircraft)

s(SS-)PzAbt *schwere (SS-)Panzer-Abteilung* = (SS-) heavy tank battalion (Tigers or King Tigers)

SSR South Saskatchewan Regt

Stp *Stützpunkt* = German strongpoint

StuG *Sturmgeschütz* = German assault gun

Tobruk German concrete MG or mortar position

Unit nomenclature: Allied – 21st Army Group, First Canadian (British/US) Army, I Canadian (British/US) Corps, 3rd Can (BR/Pol/US) Div, Regt, 5th Bn/Sqn, B Coy, 2nd Pl
German – Heeresgruppe A, First Armee, I. Korps, 6. Panzer-Division, Fallschirmjäger-Abteilung/ Regiment 6, II. (Bataillon) or 2. (Kompanie)/FJR 6,

Vf *Verstärkt Feldmässig* = German strengthened field fortification

VGD *Volksgrenadier-Division* = German People's rifle division. A late war designation, most VGDs were built around a cadre of experienced officers and NCOs

Volkssturm People's militia made up of men and boys who weren't serving officially

WN *Widerstandsnest* = German defensive position

Only one tank survived in the front line from D-Day to VE-Day. Sherman III 'Bomb' entered the fray on the afternoon of 6 June with the Sherbrooke Fusilier Regt (today part of the Sherbrooke Hussars) at Bernières-sur-Mer. Today it sits outside the William Street Armoury in Sherbrooke, Quebec. Note the 53 denoting the junior regiment of the 2nd Can Armd Bde.

INDEX